Praise for

MORE IS MORE
and BLAKE MORGAN

"Every executive gives lip service to great customer service, some even have sincere intentions; but the troops thin out a bit when it comes down to actually delivering an exceptional customer experience. *More Is More* is a much deserved—and very practical—anvil to the head to anyone in business who desires to differentiate by truly amazing the customer."

—John Venhuizen, President & CEO, Ace Hardware Corp

"To be successful in today's hyper competitive marketplace, winning companies foster a culture of innovation that is laser focused on constantly enhancing long-term customer relationships. With real-life examples and highly readable prose, Blake provides a template to achieve this goal. If you are looking for more—read customer experience guru Blake Morgan's book!"

—Chris McCann, CEO 1-800-Flowers.com, Inc.

"A must read for any Chief Customer Officer! *More Is More* provides new insights into the ever-evolving field of customer experience."

—Claire Burns, Chief Customer Officer, MetLife

"Blake Morgan cuts through the customer experience hype and provides you with practical examples you can immediately implement at your organization. Read this book!"

—Darren Pleasance, Managing Director,
Global Customer Acquisitions, Google

"Blake simplifies customer experience for her readers. Want a clear-cut approach to improving customer experience through self-service, machine learning and automation? Read this book!"

—Andreas von der Heydt, Director of Kindle, Amazon

"Blake Morgan sees the future of what great customer experiences will be, and outlines how you can lead your company there."
—John Rossman, Author of *The Amazon Way: 14 Leadership Principles of the World's Most Disruptive Company*

"*More Is More* is a great collection of case studies, customer research and recommendations that will get your brain buzzing on how to take your organization's customer experience to the next level."
—James Staten, Chief Strategist, Microsoft Cloud

"Don't get disrupted! *More Is More* can give you practical tips to reexamine and reinvigorate your organization's approach to understanding and serving your customers' needs."
—Zoher Karu, Chief Data Officer, eBay

"Customer experience is a never-ending race to create meaningful interactions. This book is the race car you need to stay ahead of the competition."
—Pete Blackshaw, Global Head of Digital and Social Media, Nestle

"In a hyper connected, knowledge sharing intelligent economy, where everyone and everything is connected, customer experience is the next battleground for business. Digital business leaders can successfully manage transformation, and accelerate growth, by positioning customer relationship management as their company's center of gravity. Blake Morgan's book is a brilliant guide for becoming a truly customer centric business."
—Vala Afshar, Chief Digital Evangelist, Salesforce

"Blake Morgan's *More Is More* makes a compelling case and provides a clear roadmap for organizations to dig deeper to deliver powerful, differentiating customer experiences."
—Peter Horst, Former CMO, The Hershey Company

"Blake Morgan uniquely understands how new technologies impact customer experience, making her one of the go-to gurus in the field today."
—Nova Spivack, Entrepreneur, Investor, Grandson of Peter Drucker

MORE
IS
MORE

MORE
IS
MORE

How the Best Companies Go Farther
and Work Harder to Create
Knock-Your-Socks-Off Customer
Experiences

BLAKE MORGAN

 bibliomotion
inc.

First edition published in 2017
by Bibliomotion, Inc.
711 Third Avenue New York, NY 10017, USA
2 Park Square, Milton Park, Abingdon, Oxon OX14 4RN, UK

© 2017 by Blake Morgan

Bibliomotion is an imprint of Taylor & Francis Group, an informa business

No claim to original U.S. Government works

Printed on acid-free paper

International Standard Book Number-13 978-1-138-04678-8 (Hardback)
International Standard Book Number-13 978-1-315-17131-9 (eBook)

Library of Congress Cataloging-in-Publication Data
A catalog record for this book has been requested

Visit the Taylor & Francis Web site at http://www.taylorandfrancis.com

Printed and bound in the United States of America by Sheridan

For Jacob, my love, my copilot.

Contents

Foreword   xi

Acknowledgments   xiii

Introduction: What Is Customer Experience—and
Why Is It Important?   xv

Part 1   The Customer Experience Today and Tomorrow   1

Chapter 1   The Current State of Customer Experience   3

Chapter 2   Customers Want to Do Business on Their Terms   15

Chapter 3   The Growing Role of Technology in Customer
Experience   27

Chapter 4   Cleaning Up a Mess of Big Data and
Marketing   41

Part 2   Creating Knock-Your-Socks-Off Customer
Experience: D.O.M.O.R.E.   55

Chapter 5   Design Something Special   57

Chapter 6   Offer a Strong Employee Experience   69

Chapter 7   Modernize With Technology   77

Chapter 8   Obsess Over the Customer   83

Chapter 9   Reward Responsibility and Accountability   93

Chapter 10 Embrace Disruption and Innovation   107

Part 3   Designing the Customer Experience of Tomorrow   121

Chapter 11 The Six Rings of the Modern Customer
                Experience   123

Chapter 12 Culture, Vision, and Priorities   135

Chapter 13 Generational Customer Experience   143

Chapter 14 Making It Right With Your Customers   159

Chapter 15 A Focus on Quarterly Profits Kills Long-Term
                Growth   171

Conclusion   177

References   179

Index   189

About the Author   197

Foreword

Creating unforgettable customer experiences can only be achieved when a company is constantly striving to do more. So, what exactly does "doing more" entail? For many of today's most forward-thinking retailers, it involves developing a deeper understanding of a customer's individual needs and preferences and then using those insights to tailor and simplify their overall shopping experience. Doing more also means leveraging emerging technologies and cutting-edge tools to transform and amplify the ways in which customers experience and interact with their favorite brands. Moreover, as Blake Morgan illustrates in this must-read book, doing more should embody a brand's desire to dig deeper, take calculated risks, and pioneer the unknown to create stand-out experiences that are genuinely unique, innovative, and memorable to their customers.

Blake Morgan, an accomplished writer, speaker, adviser, and one of the most knowledgeable experts in the Customer Experience field, preaches this narrative to perfection in *More Is More*, providing invaluable insights, sharing actionable advice, and drawing from real-world examples in challenging today's business leaders to place the customer experience in the forefront.

I first met Blake when she reached out to me after reading about my company's focus on revolutionizing the customer experience: specifically, our early-mover initiatives into the fast-evolving world of conversational commerce that leverage machine learning and artificial intelligence, such as Facebook's bots and Amazon's Alexa platform. Blake graciously invited me to participate in "The Modern Customer" podcast that she was hosting. During our discussions, I quickly discovered that she has an incredibly inquisitive mind combined with a rare ability to shape her insights and deliver them in concise, actionable language.

In *More Is More*, Blake points out that, while many brands have differing priorities, those that are committed to an unwavering focus on their customers and creating thoughtful, one-of-a-kind campaigns that appeal to them are not only getting noticed, but also thriving in an increasingly complex digital landscape. Blake's advice: instead of being intimidated and shying away from the abundance of new channels and digital platforms, brands need to act quickly and figure out meaningful strategies that can help them meet potential customers at these new touch points.

More Is More proves beyond a doubt that, contrary to popular belief, the customer experience boils down to far more than just sales and customer service. Blake highlights the immeasurable importance of several other factors, including management, product innovation, user experience, customer and brand journey, post purchase relationship, and much more. Brands that consider all of these factors in their digital strategy are leaps and bounds ahead of their competitors, who are still trying to emerge from the middle of the pack and win a larger market share. Whether she's advising how companies can leverage technology, dishing on why brands need to be putting big data to use, warning of the detriments of a disconnected employee experience or breaking down her signature D.O.M.O.R.E. and Six Rings of the Modern Customer Experience models, Blake Morgan's *More Is More* is an absolute must-read for brand leaders and virtually anyone else who hopes to survive and thrive in today's customer-driven commerce landscape.

Chris McCann
CEO, 1-800-Flowers.com, Inc.

Acknowledgments

I've been writing since I was seven years old. Although I was never a great test taker, when I entered my freshman year, my mom went to the school and vehemently requested my placement into honors English. Mom, thank you for always believing in me. You modeled independence and creativity for me, and this shaped a lot of my hunger to look at the world differently than I was told to. Dad, I want to acknowledge you for taking me to basketball games just like you did my older brother. Thank you for giving me the nickname of Terminator when I was a twelve-year-old girl on the soccer field, and for teaching me to get back up when I'm kicked down. To both of my parents: I have newfound respect for you now that I'm a mom. To my daughter, Naomi: I wrote this book while very pregnant with you—thank you for being a good girl and motivating me to work. I want to thank my husband, Jacob Morgan. We are lucky in that we choose to spend all of our time together and we have for seven years. Every year just gets better. We live, work, and play side by side. You always encourage me to get out of my comfort zone. Then, when I am inevitably uncomfortable, you make me laugh and make it all better. We are on this journey together, and with each year, I love you more. Thank you to my brother, Justin, my Dad's partner Cheryl, and my entire extended family.

I want to thank Erika Heilman for giving me this opportunity. Thank you Susan Lauzau for being a patient editor, and Michael Sinocchi for managing the editorial process. I'd like to thank Fred Allen and Vicky Valet over at *Forbes*. Thank you to my clients for giving me opportunities so I can continue to do what I love. Lastly, thank you to the customer experience community for reading, watching, and sharing my content. This is a great industry, and so are all the people in it.

INTRODUCTION

What Is Customer Experience— and Why Is It Important?

The first official customers on record existed in 6,000 BCE. Those were Mesopotamian participants in bartering, the earliest known form of trade.[1] Today, most people don't barter: they buy. And things today look a little different. Technology plays an important role in the life of a modern customer—many prefer to communicate via their thumbs, sending a snap, rather than by using their vocal cords to make a call.

While customer–company exchanges may look very different than they once did, the premise of such transactions is similar: each party has something the other wants, and they work out a deal to trade items. Today, however, we can find the product that best meets our needs with the click of a button. Via technology such as augmented reality apps, we can even try on a lipstick without going to the makeup counter. In fact, modern customers can get just about anything, anytime, anywhere. Today, selling is not just about the product or service on offer. The sales transaction itself is now just one small piece of customer experience. To stay in business, companies need to understand what customer experience is and how they can create rich customer experiences that work to their advantage.

You know the phrase "less is more"? It may be true about many things, but it's not true when it comes to customer experience. Companies that want to stay relevant must apply more energy, focus, and resources to creating knock-your-socks-off customer experiences than they ever did before. The companies that embrace a "more is more" philosophy work harder and go further to ensure that their customers have a positive experience. Companies that understand the importance of a relationship—even one individual relationship—are willing to go to any length to ensure that they continue to nurture that relationship. They do this through customer-focused strategies and leadership, via operations, policies, and procedures that consider how the customer will fare in every scenario.

Companies that refuse to invest in making their organizations customer-centric continue to cut the resources needed to create compelling customer experiences. These are the companies that will not survive the commoditization of their products and services. The companies that now rise to the top simply do more to avoid being lost in a sea of sameness among their competition.

Today's Complex Digital Environment

Here's the first reason that most customer experiences are not making the cut: a majority of companies do not have the culture and attitude necessary to create compelling customer experiences. Customer experience is an attitude embraced within the company; it's a company-wide approach to building an operation that has the customer at its center. Not purely customer service, customer experience starts much earlier than the point at which the customer engages. It is baked into a company's products and services, created by everyone who works for or with the company, including vendor partners or the third party that delivers the final product or service. Everything your company does impacts customers' perceptions of their relationship with your brand—that is, the customer experience.

More Is More provides practical advice for building or improving customer experience that you can apply immediately at your own organization. Time is of the essence. Your customers are not willing to wait for you to get the customer experience right. In this book, I'll show you the invisible toxins that are killing your customer experience and your market share, and I'll show you how to address them.

Today's digital environment is increasingly complex. Customers are using new channels faster than brands can establish a presence on those channels, and by the time a brand has mastered engagement on one channel, customers are onto the next one. While some brands struggle to create a meaningful digital experience for customers, others have missed the boat completely. The past few years have seen one big box retailer after the other disappear, as the Internet has destroyed some businesses and given birth to many others. Given the increasingly complex digital landscape, it's difficult to know where a brand can even start. *More Is More* sets you up for success, outlining the key areas you need to address immediately so you can weather external changes, remain relevant, and thrive in the ever-changing business landscape.

The idea that customers are valuable and should be treated well so they come back is not new. We've been talking about it for decades. So why are we still having the same conversations, year after year? My theory is that boards and CEOs refuse to focus on long-term gains because they are shackled by the pressure of quarterly profits. The pressure to produce more with less and do it faster has an unfortunate effect on the way resources are allocated. Generally, sales and marketing are the first departments to receive resources, and other areas of the business that affect customer experiences are an afterthought. Many of us who advocate for customers within our organizations, and those of us who have frustrating experiences as customers, are still banging our heads against the wall. In many organizations, nothing has changed in the last thirty years: customer experience remains an afterthought. *Easy*, *simple*, and *painless* are not words generally associated with customer experience. If you are a person in modern society, then you have likely had a terrible customer experience in the recent past. It's unavoidable.

Misconceptions about what compels customers to come back abound. Customers do not come back just because you offer the cheapest product. They don't flock to you because you have the flashiest marketing campaign. The reason customers come back? Because you provide a superior product or service, and you do it in a way that makes customers' lives better and easier. Let's consider a modern truth: brands need to create beautifully simple and easy customer experiences. The easier you can make life for your customers at the outset, the less likely it is that you will need to do damage control after a sale. That means your products must work like they're supposed to, that the end product you provide to the customer has been fully vetted, and that every possible problem scenario has been evaluated. Most companies continue to provide half-baked products and services, and as a result, they spend a lot of time fixing things for customers after the fact.

Internal processes and operations are broken and are so unfriendly to the customer that damage control is an everyday reality for most companies. Unfortunately, many companies have accepted this mediocre state and feel powerless to change it; instead, they've set up customer service departments to address customer concerns after the fact. But what if the experience was so simple, so smart, and so consistent that we didn't need customer service anymore? I'm talking about a company that is so good it doesn't have unhappy customers contacting it. This is a fantasy world, of course. Even the highest-performing companies have customer hiccups. It's an unavoidable part of life. Your customers are human beings, and human beings will always have unique issues that need to be addressed. And even with the best of intentions, things go wrong, whether it's due to company error or customer error. However, we've created and settled for business systems that are toxic—and instead of fixing the system, we are focused on being firefighters. We have a mentality that "things break down, and we have a department for when they do." I suggest that you instead spend more time developing better core systems to make life easier for your company and better for your customers.

Let's talk about why customer experiences often fall short. One reason is that the people who make the product are disconnected from the people who consume the product. While some companies enjoy the benefits of highly collaborative and open environments, many still operate as though we are at the beginning of the Industrial Revolution. One group is responsible for making one piece of the product, another group is responsible for another, and the many groups that pass the products or service down the line don't interact. A disconnected customer experience is the result of a disconnected employee experience. Companies that operate like this do not orbit around the customers—the customers orbit around the company. If every employee

Figure 0.1 *Customer Experience*

who was involved with the creation of the product had more insight into the customer who uses the product, those employees would understand how to make better products.

Brands are in such a rush to produce and make profits that they're not slowing down to put the entire company into orbit around the customer. As habits expert Gretchen Rubin says, they are not "going slow to go fast."[2] Companies need to take more time up front to think intelligently about the customer who will use the product—and what that experience actually should be. An unfortunate reality is that most employees—whether these employees are leaders or not—have no idea what the customer's experience is like.

Going Slow to Go Fast

Companies would benefit greatly from considering how every single decision affects the customer experience. They would be wildly successful if only they had a constant reminder of the customer's presence in every meeting. Companies are missing the boat when it comes to the full customer experience, including advertising, packaging, product and service features, ease of use, and reliability. They are missing key steps to building robust customer experiences and, as a result, they rely on damage control. Here's why: organizations are terrified to slow down and be thoughtful.

Companies face increasing pressure to perform on a quarterly basis, and the race to hit financial marks does not leave room for anything but the making of products and services. There is no time for anyone to stop and think about *how* the sausages are made. But as we rush to produce more, faster, we are leaving important ingredients out of the recipe. We are missing important steps that will improve the customer experience by leaps and bounds. To create better products, companies need to slow down and think about their approach. However, they feel they can't slow down until they make a certain amount in profits, and that won't happen until the approach changes, creating a catch-22. We need to stop and think about how we're doing what we're doing—and, most importantly, why!

Let's Talk About Time

Most of us feel like we don't have a lot of time. We work more than nine to five, then we add two hours a day for commuting. The average person gets up between 6 and 6:30 a.m. to ready the kids for school and get to work on time.[3] They work all day with little personal time to take care of life's emergencies. Some people work until 6 p.m. and get home around 7 p.m. Then it's time for dinner and to spend the precious few leftover minutes with the kids before bed. There's your day. It's 9 p.m. before the only "me time" most people have begins.

I'm painting this picture because this is you *and* this is your customer. You are both trying to do what you can to live a somewhat balanced life. Most of us don't have time in our lives for things to break. When we choose to do business with a company, we need those products and services to function 100 percent of the time, so we can continue to sustain our lives. If you can be a company that is different because you have compassion and think about your customers' lives outside your "doors," you will attract a greater following. We know that today most companies don't think about the reality of customers' lives. If they were compassionate toward the plight of their customers, they would create experiences for customers that made their lives easier, not harder. If more employees within companies thought about what they were taking away from customers by not being customer-centric, they would change the way they worked. They wouldn't treat customers like numbers on spreadsheets.

How This Book Will Help: D.O.M.O.R.E.

In this book, I explore the concept of D.O.M.O.R.E. The company that operates by these principles

DESIGNS something special
OFFERS a strong employee experience

MODERNIZES with technology
OBSESSES over the customer
REWARDS responsibility and accountability
EMBRACES disruption and innovation

Figure 0.2 shares the six aspects of a company that simply does more. Today, the brand that is competitive is the one that literally does more. These competitive brands are not only providing something unique to customers, but they have a laser focus on doing "more" in every aspect of the company. They do more by treating employees well, by building a robust technology offering for those employees, and by creating a strong company culture. In this book, I provide examples of the ways some of the top companies are

ESIGNS something special

FFERS a strong employee experience

ODERNIZES with technology

BSESSES over the customer

EWARDS responsibility and accountability

MBRACES disruption and innovation

BLAKEMORGAN
www.blakemichellemorgan.com

Figure 0.2 *D.O.M.O.R.E.*

going above and beyond, and I pull out the most important pieces to show you what you can learn from these leaders.

Doing more for your customers is the only way to make sure your company will be around even next year. The rise and collapse of businesses happens at an alarming rate. Just as quickly as a company achieves success, it can disappear overnight. Markets are moving faster than at any point in history, and it's up to you to determine whether you want to focus on improvements now or wait until you are no longer relevant. *More Is More* gives you the ideas and inspiration you need to get to work improving your customer experience today. If you want to be the company that dazzles, that makes headlines, and that stands out from the crowd, it's not too late. You can start improving your customer experience today simply by reading this book and using the tools I provide at your own organization. Let's take this ride together. By the end of our journey, you will have more than a few ideas to get you on the road to offering a knock-your-socks-off customer experience.

Notes

1. "Barter System History, the Past and the Present," *Mint.com*, December 7, 2016.
2. "Podcast 64: Go Slow to Go Fast; What Do You Lie About; and a New Segment–the 'Happiness Hack.'" *The Happiness Project*, last modified May 11, 2016, http://gretchenrubin.com/happiness_project/2016/05/podcast-64/.
3. Meg Lazovick, "Wake Me Up: What Time Do Americans Start Their Day?" *Edison Research*, March 26, 2015, accessed July 3, 2016, www.edisonresearch.com/wake-me-up-series-2/.

PART 1

The Customer Experience Today and Tomorrow

Let's establish something; most companies have the best of intentions. When they open their doors, most businesses are ready and willing to help customers solve their most pressing problems. However, as time goes on and profits become more and more important, something gets lost. The business makes a sacrifice in service here, allows a decrease in quality there—and before you know it, the customer experience has gone downhill. Over time, the small and eager company has turned into a big machine and lost its way.

A company has a bad habit of acting like a flaky person you're dating. At first the suitor works very hard to win you over. He picks you up on time, brings you flowers, and promises you a wonderful life together. You fall in love, give him a set of keys to your apartment, and tell your family and friends about him. You change your Facebook status. But, in time, he stops bringing flowers, stops showing up on time for your dates, and eventually stops calling. He doesn't even text. Companies are guilty of similar bad behavior. In the beginning, they work hard to get your attention and your business. They make promises about what life will look like once you use their products. But after you've been seduced by the promises, they don't want to hear from you. They don't want to spend a lot of time nurturing the relationship, making sure you're happy and engaged. The attitude of these companies is, "Wham, bam, thank you, ma'am."

Some companies, though, see how successful they can be when they put as much effort into the customer experience throughout the relationship as they did in the beginning. This book is the best dating manual you will ever read, but from a business perspective.

In part 1, we'll look at the current state of customer experience, the desire of customers to do business on their own terms, and the growing role technology plays in customer experience.

CHAPTER 1

The Current State of Customer Experience

Have you noticed that most people don't listen? Think about the dinner parties you go to. Do you find that people ask you a lot of questions, or does it seem that most people genuinely like to talk about themselves? In business, the failure to understand what customers need, or what their experience is, represents the worst offense against customers. Salespeople who talk at customers and don't listen to what customers need are among the worst offenders.

Listening is hard. It requires an individual to focus and control her urge to talk over the other person. Why do people and companies make the mistake of not listening? Mostly, because it feels good to talk. As humans, we enjoy expressing ourselves, conveying messages, and feeling heard. Listening can be scary. When you ask someone what he wants from you—rather than telling him what he should want—you leave room for the other person to ask for something you can't deliver. You (the seller) risk not having what the person wants. You could hear no.

Businesses need to be listening every single day because what customers are saying is changing at an increasingly frequent pace. While many companies are listening closely, many are not. In fact, many marketers are using the approach they've always used. In a recent Ernst & Young survey on the C-suite perspective, only 31 percent of the 800 C-level executives surveyed said the CMO drove the best marketing practices tailored to constantly changing customers.[1] That means that about only one-third of CMOs listen to and understand customers. The CMO is a key player within the company impacting the customer experience—this should be a major alarm to every CEO today.

A Treasure Trove of Information From Customers

We're living at a time when there is more free and easily obtained feedback than there has been at any time in the history of the world. We have constant access to a treasure trove of insight about our products, neighboring products, and pretty much anything else we want to know about.

When you read feedback about products, services, or experiences on Amazon, Yelp, or Trip Advisor, you see that consumers are generally complaining that the product or service did not meet their expectations. In his book *Customer Experience 3.0*, John Goodman talks about the fact that customers are more upset with brands when they feel duped or misled about a product than they are by any other part of the customer experience. More than anything, customers dislike the feeling that you—the brand—assume they are stupid. One of the ways brands do this is by creating one-size-fits-all approaches; by treating customers as if they are all the same, brands end up looking sloppy, with products and services that aren't relevant for many customers. Perhaps some customers' needs go unmet altogether. Most customer experiences are created for the masses. One message is sent via a television ad, billboard, or another traditional channel. The point is to reach as many people as possible in one swoop. One message is created for hundreds of thousands of people, sometimes millions. In your own life, you wouldn't talk to everyone you come across in the same way. You probably wouldn't say the same thing to everyone. Why? Because much of the information wouldn't be relevant for everyone you spoke with. But this is precisely what companies do today.

Customers seek personalized, relevant, and just-in-time messaging. It's time to move from lazy, one-size-fits-all messaging to tailored, relevant messaging. This is easier said than done, however, and not many companies are doing a good job at it. The way you communicate with your customers has an immense impact on the experience they have. Brands are no longer defined by a single marketing message, but by the daily interactions the customer has with the brand.

There is a customer experience crisis unfolding, and brands don't seem to know how to fix it. No matter how many articles and books are published, how many studies are conducted, or how many customers complain on social media, brands are still at a loss about how to improve. Even with brands' unprecedented access to better tools across the organization, mediocrity in customer experience remains the norm.

Mediocrity is everywhere. The brands that don't pay greater attention to the customer experience will not be around for much longer, and commoditization is the reason these brands will die. Matthew Dixon, Nick Toman, and Rick Delisi write in their book *The Effortless Experience: Conquering the New Battleground for Customer Loyalty,*

> Commoditization, not just of products but of brand promises, is one of the unavoidable hard truths of doing business in the twenty-first century. The time from launch to peak of market acceptance to everyone else ripping off your great new idea and calling it their own is shrinking down to almost nothing.[2]

As soon as you think you have something that sets your brand apart, competitors launch an identical product or service or claim. According to a study conducted by the authors, customers view only 20 percent of corporate brands as "truly differentiated." Most offerings are very similar, and the bar isn't set very high because most brands don't execute well on customer experience.

A brand that is not fully in control of the total customer experience must vet its resellers and partners so that the final product or service is delivered seamlessly. If your company sells appliances, for example, you need to ensure that the delivery and installation company you subcontract to holds itself to the same standards that your brand embraces. When the delivery company's employees go into customers' houses, are they professional? Are they personable? Do they reek of cigarette smoke? These things matter.

My husband and I just moved into a new house, and almost every single purchase we made had some kind of problem, from issues with the purchase and installation of shutters to problems getting furniture delivered and getting the house painted. Even beloved electronics giant Best Buy delivered a flawed TV four times. The delivery person would install the flat-screen TV on our wall and turn the TV on, and a purple dot would glare back at us. Another company tried to deliver a couch and thought we wouldn't notice the huge tear in the fabric. When we went to return the item, the customer service representative told us the company was being bought and would not be able to make any transactions for weeks, maybe longer. Our experience with this particular company got so bad that we asked our bank to use fraud protection to get our money back. Now, that is incompetence you can't even dream up! Everyone you talk with has stories like these that illustrate the level of dysfunction in our everyday service interactions.

Someone Must Own Customer Experience

For a customer experience program to be effective, the most senior leaders at the company must take ownership of the program. But unless the CEO appoints a chief customer officer, a chief customer experience officer, or even a chief marketing officer who is empowered to get things done for the customer, it's hard to say who will lobby for the customer across the organization. While it's wonderful to have a CEO who takes on customer experience, without focus, the priority can be lost among a sea of pressures. Research from companies like PricewaterhouseCoopers (PwC) shows that 63 percent of CEOs want to rally their organizations around the customer as a top investment priority, but that is easier said than done.[3]

The problem can generally be traced by to budgets and priorities. Worldwide, brands spend $500 billion per year on marketing and advertising and a mere $9 billion per year on customer service.[4] A report by vendor Genesys and the Economist Intelligence Unit shows there's frequent confusion over who is truly responsible for the customer experience.[5] The report, published in June of 2015, surveyed 516 senior-level executives from twenty-one countries. The vast majority of these (464) were C-suite executives—of whom 165 were CEOs—while the remaining fifty-two respondents were heads of a business unit. According to the study, two in three companies surveyed (63 percent) say that customer experience is a "very important" investment priority. Two in five companies (42 percent) have boosted relevant spending by more than 10 percent in the past three years, a proportion that is estimated to climb to more than half (51 percent) over the next three years (by 2018).

Clearly, businesses believe that customer experience matters. But do they act on it? That depends on who owns it. When it comes to the big question, "Who owns customer experience?" the most successful companies have a CEO who takes ownership of it. The study showed that 58 percent of companies that say they are much more profitable than their competitors report that the CEO is in charge of customer experience. Only 37 percent of less profitable companies say the same. Meaning, if you have a CEO who cares deeply about customer experience and takes it on, your company is going to reap the benefits.

Companies that fail to respond to these changing modes of communication are vulnerable to large-scale customer flight.[6] Not only that, but the study points to increased competition and the fact that, because of the greater number of service channels, the potential for customer dissatisfaction is also higher. What is telling about the study is the overall lack of accountability when it comes to customer experience. When asked who is leading customer experience transformation initiatives, CEOs say one thing and those who work for them say something different. Seventy-two percent of CEOs say they (the CEO) are in charge of customer experience, but only 27 percent of the other executives surveyed agree that the CEO is in charge of that area.

No wonder customer experiences are, by and large, far from ideal. Too many people are claiming partial ownership over the customer experience, and as a result, nothing is getting done. Smart CEOs who don't have adequate time to commit to customer experience are delegating, with some of the most forward-thinking companies appointing a chief customer officer, who has real authority to get things done across the organization.

The Importance of a Chief Customer Officer

The chief customer officer represents the customer at the highest levels of the organization. Some chief customer officers are responsible for account management and customer service, while other chief customer officers are free agents who liaise with various departments across the company. Ideally, the chief customer officer spends a lot of time with customers and takes the customer feedback and insights to every department. That way, the entire company is on the same page around customer experience. The more visibility the chief customer officer has across the company, the better. One of the goals of the chief customer officer is to structure the company around the customer. Organizational structure and hierarchy are not the same at every company, however, and some companies may have various influential positions, such as VP of customer experience, chief experience officer, or other more creative titles.

In 2015, the CCO Council's *Annual Chief Customer Officer Study* showed continued growth in the number of CCOs at major corporations, with 10 percent of Fortune 500 companies having already adopted the role, a percentage that jumps to 22 percent among the Fortune 100.[7]

The more profitable the company, the more likely it is to have a chief customer officer at the helm. At big companies, it can be hard to get things done, and one highly influential person with budget authority and freedom to move across the organization can cut through much of the bureaucracy. Jeanne Bliss, author of *Chief Customer Officer*, calls this position the "human duct tape" of the organization. In her book, she quotes the former chief marketing officer and customer experience officer of Walgreens, Graham Atkinson: "The role of the CCO is to drive executive appetite for wanting to know the interruptions in customer's lives, simplifying how they are delivered and facilitating a one-company response to these key operational performance areas."[8] This is a smart way to describe the role of the CCO. Driving executive appetite for learning about customers' lives is not easy. How do you get the busiest people within the company to put top priority on something they can't see every day (customers)? Additionally, how do you get the entire company to care about the many inconveniences and interruptions created in customers' lives by poor customer experiences? Bliss says that if you reduce or eliminate these interruptions for customers, your business will always thrive.

Involving the Whole Company

The reality of customer experience is that everyone in the company owns it. Unfortunately, because of culture issues, employees often don't realize that they have a palpable impact on the customer's experience. Amazing companies have a culture of excellence, but these are few and far between. Face it, it's hard to achieve a customer-centric culture because it takes effort—especially from leadership—and most leaders don't want to exert the requisite energy. The CEO must lead by example, sending a message to everyone in the company that customers and the customer experience are of the utmost importance. Here's an important attribute of a high-performing company: senior leadership doesn't hide in their offices. It's critical that senior leadership get out to the "floor," so to speak, and engage with employees as visible examples of the company's values.

There is no better example of CEOs engaging with employees in this way than the TV show *Undercover Boss*. Episode after episode shows a CEO going undercover to find out what it's really like in the underbelly of the company. Most of the time, thanks to expert makeup and hair styling, these executives go undetected. In almost every episode, there's a huge disconnect between what the CEO (who is undercover) believes is happening at the company and what is actually happening. Employees do not always embrace the values that the CEO believes all employees accept, and sometimes an employee actually gets fired for bad behavior. After all, these employees don't realize they are communicating with the CEO of the company, and they let their hair down, for better or worse. Not an episode goes by that the CEO doesn't learn something surprising—sometimes for the better, but often for the worse.

This gap between what people at the top of the company believe is happening and what is actually happening often has to do with customer-centricity. In *Undercover Boss*, we see some employees show the care they take in their role. Examples include frontline employees who wear big grins and display can-do attitudes. As a result, their customers love them, which is clear from the video footage. If only every CEO had the chance to appear on *Undercover Boss*! But in some respects, they do: all CEOs can spend time with their frontline employees and customers, learning in a hands-on way how the business of the organization moves forward. However, many CEOs don't make the time to walk the floor or to understand every piece of the business that affects the customer.

Corporate Structure Doesn't Set Customer Experience Up for Success

When you have the opportunity to peek under the hood of a large company, you will generally find that the employee experience matches the customer experience. If the customer experience is disjointed, employee experience is often the same. At medium-sized or large companies that outsource pieces of the customer experience, there may be a lack of solid collaboration among the core team. A different person is likely responsible for each piece of customer care; for example, one person runs customer relations management, one person runs social media, one person manages the call centers, and so on. Completely different vendors may handle different channels for the company; for example, one vendor handles live chat, e-mail, and communities, while another vendor handles phone, social media (such as Facebook and Twitter), and any contacts that come in through the website. Another vendor handles the internal collaboration software or knowledge base used by employees to communicate about customers and customer issues.

The people who "own" these different outsourced functions may not work in the same building, and they may rarely talk. They do, however, meet with a common boss perhaps once every two weeks, and that boss is somehow supposed to enable seamlessness across functions. Now consider the fact that the agencies that run the social media marketing promotions never interact with anyone on the customer service team. There are no mandates given by the top for employees to collaborate among these different groups. Sure, the company might have internal communities that run on Jive, Lithium, or Salesforce, but the siloes that play out in the real world continue on these internal networks.

I've just presented the reality of working at a big company. Now consider the fact that there are many different business units that are also operating in their own silo. It sounds like a real mess, doesn't it? When a customer does business with various areas of an organization and the experiences feel completely disparate, it's because that's precisely how those experiences are built inside the company: there are matching disparate employee experiences.

Brands Are Much Worse Drivers Than They Think They Are

Most people think they are better drivers than they actually are. There's a name for this: illusory superiority,[9] and it's a cognitive bias that leads people to overestimate their own qualities and abilities, relative to others'. But it's not just people who believe they are better drivers than they are in reality. Brands do this too!

Brands are driving, and they're not looking in the back seat to check on their passengers. The customers get out of the car and think, "I will never take this ride ever again!" The drivers have no idea until one day they look back to see an empty seat. Think about your own life: When was the last time you had an experience with a brand that was so good you had a smile on your face afterward? But I'll bet you can easily recall a customer experience that made you want to pull your hair out. The problem is that so many brands today are complacent. Complacency is the feeling of being satisfied with the way things are and not working to improve. Brands today don't have the luxury of coasting on their reputations. Complacency is a killer, and nowhere is it more evident than in the customer experience.

In the last few years, complacency has killed entire industries overnight. New companies are eager and hungry. They are sprouting up all over the world, and they know they can't rest on their laurels. Think of some of the innovative companies coming out of the sharing economy and eating industries that have been around for fifty years. The sharing economy encompasses a range of companies that provide economic arrangements in which people mutualize access to products or services rather than having individual ownership. The phenomenon stems from an increasing consumer desire to be in control of consumption instead of being "passive 'victims' of hyperconsumption."[10]

In the past few decades, we've gone from a consumer culture to one that is moving in the other direction, toward an anti-consumerist philosophy. Younger generations are refraining from buying a house, owning a car, or dropping their life savings on material goods. These young people value access over ownership. While companies operating in the sharing economy—TaskRabbit or Rover, for example—can do their best to provide parameters and governance for customer-facing contractors or employees—errand runners or dog walkers—the companies are not fully in control of the entire customer journey. They make up for what they can't control with solid engineering of the customer's journey via technology. Customers are willing to overlook what these sharing economy companies lack in streamlined operations because of their unparalleled offerings (price, control over options, and convenience).

Many large traditional companies make the mistake of thinking they can mold their employees to act as robotic extensions of the brand. Individual employees are beaten down with a series of no's until they conform to the culture of the brand—and the brand thinks this will help create systematic processes and operations. But you do not want employees who behave like robots—that is counter to the culture you want to create. Successful companies need employees who can think on their feet and make decisions without constant oversight. The more you create a culture of self-governance, the more your employees will be able to make sound decisions on the fly and do right by the customer. Your employees' feelings about their work have an immense impact on the actual service or product you're making or selling.

***

Most companies have overcomplicated many parts of their business, and this unnecessary complexity makes it difficult for the company to accomplish small tasks for the customer. This is a problem because customers don't have the patience to wait for companies to "un-complicate" themselves. Consider the fact that customers are busier than ever. Modern life has sped up the expectations for everyone, not just you. Customers seek to do business with companies that make their lives easier so they can spend their time doing the things they *actually want* to do.

Notes

1. EY, *Competition, Coexistence or Symbiosis? The DNA of C-Suite Sales and Marketing Leaders the CMO Perspective*, p. 5 (London: EY, 2014).
2. Matthew Dixon, Nick Toman, and Rick Delisi, *The Effortless Experience: Conquering the New Battleground for Customer Loyalty*, p. 6 (London: Penguin/Portfolio, 2013).
3. Shayla Price, "Why Customer-Focused Content Should Be a Priority," *Marketing Media Insider*, February 15, 2016, https://marketinginsidergroup.com/content-marketing/customer-focused-content-priority/.
4. Kayla Brehm, "7 Facts That Show That Customer Service Is More Profitable Than Sales." *Help.com*, September 22, 2014, https://blog.help.com/2014/09/22/7-facts-that-show-that-customer-service-is-more-profitable-than-sales.
5. "The Value of Experience: How the C-Suite Values Customer Experience in the Digital Age Global & North America Executive Summary,"

Genesys, November 19, 2016, www.genesys.com/about/resources/the-value-of-experience-how-the-c-suite-values-customer-experience-in-the-digital-age-na.

6. Genesys, Economist Intelligence Unit Report: The Value of Experience, How The C-Suite Values Customer Experience in The Digital Age, 2016, December 7, 2016.

7. Ashley Friedlein, "Chief Customer Officers (CCOs): A Fad or the Future?" *Econsultancy*, October 12, 2015, https://econsultancy.com/blog/67031-chief-customer-officers-ccos-a-fad-or-the-future/.

8. Blake Morgan, "Seven Questions With Customer Strategy Expert, Jeanne Bliss," Forbes, June 8, 2015, http://www.forbes.com/sites/blakemorgan/2015/06/08/sevenquestionswithcustomerstrategyexpertjeannebliss/2/?ss=leadership#29ed49f690b5.

9. *Wikipedia*, s.v. "Illusory Superiority," last modified October 4, 2016, https://en.wikipedia.org/wiki/Illusory_superiority.

10. Juho Hamari, Mimmi Sjöklint, and Antti Ukkonen, "The Sharing Economy: Why People Participate in Collaborative Consumption," *Journal of the Association for Information Science and Technology* 67, no. 9 (2015): 2047–2059, doi:10.1002/asi.23552.

CHAPTER 2

Customers Want to Do Business on Their Terms

Five major trends are shaping the future of customer experience, and these are (1) changing expectations and customer behavior, (2) technology, (3) the on-demand and sharing economies, (4) data, and (5) organizational design. In the next few chapters, I will break these five trends down for you and explain how they are relevant to you and your company's future.

Let's talk first about customer expectations and why they are changing so rapidly. A customer's expectations are set by her previous experiences with a company and also by her experiences with other companies, which serve as constant comparisons. Can you imagine how a customer who uses Amazon compares it with an airline, a utility company, or the DMV? Customers' standards change as their expectations are exceeded by new and innovative brands. For example, after Amazon Prime became popular, online customers expected not only free shipping but free returns. Almost overnight, Amazon completely reshaped customers' expectations around what should be free and what should be paid for. And similar disruptions are occurring across nearly every industry, as upstarts seek competitive advantage in a crowded market.

How can brands that want to operate the same way they always have expect to stay relevant? The tastes, preferences, and basic assumptions of their buyers are changing. When buyers interact with brands today, those customers largely do not have the convenience, ease of use, and simplicity that they enjoy with technology in their personal lives. While most companies still don't create compelling digital and mobile experiences for customers, customers want to interact with brands in the same easy way they communicate with their family and friends. If your company does not provide a strong digital and mobile experience, you are in real trouble.

You know how it's hard to go on vacation with a large group because everyone has his or her own priorities? Companies face similar challenges in improving customer experiences: it's tough to herd a group toward a common goal. Many of today's companies have gotten so big that every department or division is off doing its own thing. The executive team needs to get the entire company aligned around the same vision, the same goal, and these should be customer-centric visions, customer-centric goals.

Customers are comparing the experience they have with companies in the on-demand or online space to the experience they have with your company. And not all new and modern companies are exempt from the business pitfalls that legacy companies face. For example, when I shop on Etsy, I'm elated to enter a marketplace of homemade goods, but then I'm disappointed when I see the prices for shipping and delivery. I might pay more to have an authentic product shipped to me, but it hurts to pay high shipping costs for a product. If Amazon were to create a thriving marketplace of homemade goods with the benefit of fast shipping, I would happily switch from Etsy to Amazon.

Not only do customers expect fast and free shipping, but they expect quick responses when they have a question or a problem. And customer problems are not confined to five days out of the week or eight hours in the day. We live in a global economy, where companies must serve customers across many time zones, and customers expect lightning-fast responses around the clock, not only during daylight hours. According to Jay Baer, author of *Hug Your Haters: How to Embrace Complaints and Keep Your Customers*, 32 percent of consumers expect a response within thirty minutes when they engage through social media channels. He also found that 57 percent of consumers expect the same response time at night and on weekends that they do during normal business hours. Companies must operate in a 24–7 world. Otherwise, they risk losing business.

It's no secret that many customers refuse to go to retail stores anymore. In fact, more customers than ever before are buying their clothes online. In

2016, Amazon's second-quarter earnings report showed a record profit of $857 million, 800 percent higher than it was in 2015. Amazon is leaving retailers like Kohl's, Nordstrom, and others in the dust. When customers are actually in stores, they are on their phones, comparison shopping.[1] They are browsing their phones on their subway commute and later purchasing products on their laptops, even in B2B e-commerce.[2] And, thanks to generation Z, the use of Snapchat and WhatsApp has ballooned. Brands need to go to where the customers are—even if the people working at the brands are not familiar with those apps.

It's not just the act of purchasing that's happening on mobile, but it's the full engagement with the brand—from browsing to bookmarking items to comparison shopping to reading reviews to asking questions in-app. And it's not only generation Z that is on their phone all the time. A Bank of America mobile consumer report says that more than half of all Americans—57 percent—say they use their phone at least once an hour during the day. In New York, that statistic jumps to 96 percent. In California, it's 88 percent. Almost three-quarters of Americans who own smartphones sleep with them, and 3 percent of people sleep holding their phone in their hand.[3] And yet some companies continue to prioritize the desktop experience over the mobile experience.

Case Study: Sephora Uses Kik to Engage With Mobile Customers

A handful of brands, retailers, and publishers, including K-Swiss, Burger King, and the *Washington Post*, are flocking to messaging apps to have one-on-one conversations with consumers. Many of these companies are now turning to chatbots—computer programs that mimic human conversation—to respond to customers, allowing them to personalize their initial interactions and direct users to the right content.[4] Sephora, for example, is the first beauty brand to debut on the messaging app Kik. Known for providing anonymity to its users, Kik allows users to register without providing a telephone number, and it prevents users from being located on the service through any information other than their chosen username. According to Kik Interactive, as of February 2016, Kik has 275 million registered users,[5] including approximately 40 percent of U.S. teenagers.[6] Now Sephora offers users on Kik the opportunity to read reviews of beauty products, recommendations, and tips, and to make purchases directly on the app. Sephora also offers a short in-app quiz and uses the results to serve up content tailored to individual tastes. Recommendations are based on the customer's age group, favorite makeup, and preferred brands.

It's important for brands to look at the major social networks and the mobile experience on those networks to learn how they can engage with their customers in valuable ways.

Customer Engagement on Snapchat

Not many companies are offering service on Snapchat—as of fall 2016, Snapchat hasn't opened up its API, which would allow Snapchat to be integrated into new technology products, as Facebook and Twitter are. However, a few brave brands have entered the fray without help from social customer service vendors. For example, a small company called iOgrapher—which provides cases, lenses, microphones, tripods, and LED lighting for mobile devices—is using Snapchat to provide service to its customers. Founder David Basulto invented the iOgrapher iPad case, which allows an ordinary iPad to be easily adapted for filmmaking. The company has garnered attention from a number of influencers including Steven Spielberg, who is reportedly a customer. Basulto told me in an interview, "There are a lot of people seeking that *one* interaction that might change their whole view of your company and you've got to take it seriously . . . we're now in a world where our customers expect answers immediately."

As of June 2016, Snapchat has surpassed Twitter in terms of the number of users the platform has each day. One hundred and fifty million people are sending snaps every day—the four-year-old messaging service has become a hugely competitive player and an important social network in the lives of millions. Valued at $18 billion as of May 2016, the company has raised $1.8 billion in funding, and Bloomberg estimates a $40 billion valuation when Snapchat goes public in early 2017.[7]

Snapchat has made communicating more of a game by letting users send annotated selfies and short videos. Have you seen animated selfies of your friend on Facebook as their large eyeballs roll and they simultaneously throw up rainbows? Snapchat launched lenses in September of 2015 and allowed brands to customize their own lenses. The platform raked in millions of dollars from this engagement feature. Sponsoring and customizing a lens can cost a brand anywhere between $300,000 and $750,000 in a single day. On Halloween of 2015, the first of these sponsored lenses appeared, commissioned by 20th Century Fox to promote *The Peanuts Movie*. The lens allowed users to take a selfie with Snoopy or to puke candy corn. A logo in the corner of the snap identified the sponsor—and benefited the film, which grossed $44 million its opening weekend.[8]

Snapchat content, such as news and live stories, disappears from the platform within twenty-four hours, giving users greater privacy because the site does not retain user posts—the social network is much more private than Facebook or Twitter, which preserves the content its users post. Young people who are nervous that they might be discriminated against when they apply for a job because of implicating photos have less to worry about with Snapchat—it's private, and content goes away in a day, unless it's archived in Snapchat Memories.

Customer-Focused Offerings With Facebook Messenger

The year 2016 was a good year for Facebook. The popular social network is doing a great job of iterating its product. In a recent *New Yorker* article titled "The End of Twitter,"[9] Joshua Topolsky applauded the company's product focus and long-term commitment to user experience. In the early years,

Facebook struggled with privacy issues and customer trust, but in the past five years, the platform has worked on building trust with customers. In contrast to Twitter, Facebook has taken a stance on abuse and is quick to act on any abuses reported. Topolsky argues that, because people must register with their real names on Facebook, the platform is much safer than many others. Lastly, the company's revenue has grown 51 percent year over year because it has successfully worked on both its mobile and ad offerings.

While there is much speculation about the future of Twitter—the company had a few prospective buyers who all walked away—and frustration with Twitter in areas like online bullying, trolls, and more, Facebook has made smart and strategic decisions. Who could have known it was a good decision to essentially split Facebook in two by separating its messenger product? Facebook Messenger was reportedly the fastest-growing app of 2015, with 900 million users per month.

In 2016, Facebook rolled out Messenger for brands, including companies like Hyatt Hotels, JackThreads, and TD Bank. These brands were happy with the rollout, and Jason Rosser, head of customer experience for popular online men's retailer JackThreads, told me about his company's use of the platform:

> The uptake has been slowly increasing and customers really like it. We offer order receipts and customer service over Facebook Messenger to make it easy for our customers to manage their relationship with us. Our goal is to build lasting relationships with customers. Facebook, by its nature, is about relationships. We're excited that emerging support channels, like Facebook Messenger and texting, will bring us closer to our customer. E-mails tend to be transactional—you send a question, you get a reply, you delete thread.
>
> Facebook Messenger and text enable the customer to see their relationship with our brand. Like a conversation with a friend, it's easy for the customer to see previous conversations and where the conversation left off between us last time we interacted. Our customers like interacting with the JackThreads customer service team. We're

fun. We're real. And we're helpful, whether they need style advice or help with an order. We're going to continue to be in all of the relevant places to engage with our customers and give them confidence in the relationship we've built.

It's clear that brands like JackThreads enjoy the relationship-building aspect of engaging on Facebook. Additionally, communication is easier for both the agent and the customer because the entire message history is right there in the message thread. Customers can ask a question, go away for three hours, and come back to continue the conversation where they left off. Technologies like live chat do not offer this flexibility.

To find out more about Facebook's strategy for strengthening its customer service platform in the future, I interviewed Frerk-Malte Feller, the former director of product for Facebook Messenger. Feller told me in a phone interview:

> Altogether, if we step back, it's clear that consumers have a preference for messaging. We have 800 million users every month. Consumers have opted for messaging for personal interactions for other means. You no longer place as many phone calls or write e-mails as you did before—messaging is the main behavior in communicating with friends, family, or coworkers. We think the same will happen with businesses—messaging is a better way to communicate. That's why we're so bullish on businesses using this channel. We want businesses to be able to have delightful interactions with their customers.

In the past, we have not seen a big customer service focus at Facebook, but with so many users on the social network the pivot absolutely makes sense. As I mentioned earlier, consumers want to engage with brands with the same ease and flexibility that they have when communicating with their friends and family.

The year 2016 was arguably the year of the chatbot. At F8, Facebook's annual developer conference, Mark Zuckerberg named one brand that launched its chatbot ahead of the event: 1-800-Flowers. A brand that has always made sure to stay ahead of the technology curve, 1-800-Flowers may have a phone number for a name, but it wants the world to know it is no longer just a toll-free number. This is a company of firsts: in the early 1980s, 1-800-Flowers was the first company to allow customers to contact it via phone to order flowers for delivery; in 1992, it became the first retail company to have an e-commerce presence on the web, partnering with AOL; and now it has made news by partnering with Facebook to offer services via chatbot.

I interviewed Chris McCann, CEO and president of 1-800-Flowers, about what the company will be offering with its new chatbot: "We began experimenting with mobile commerce in 2008 and embracing different things in the social world. We now see mobile in its early stages transforming the customer experience." This chatbot will allow businesses to deliver automated customer support, e-commerce guidance, content, and interactive experiences. McCann told me,

> We learned in the early days that technology will change consumer behavior. If we're not embracing technology and change, we will be a business left behind. We look at technology and embracing change as a way to constantly reinvent our business.

1-800-Flowers is a brand built around the telephone number, and now customers don't have to call—which is wise, considering customers today spend more than three hours a day on their phone doing non-voice activities. In fact, it's incorrect to call a smartphone a phone—it's a device![10]

Facebook Messenger is also set up to completely change the way customers perform tasks such as banking. A recent article in *Venture Beat* shows how customers will now be able to complete many tasks via the Facebook Messenger bot, tasks they previously had to arrange with their bank. In the past, sending money to peers was a big headache, but now anyone can send money via Facebook Messenger simply by typing, "Send $200 to Jill Wordsworth" in a message to the bank. If Jill Wordsworth is on your list of payees, the bank will know who she is and which account the money should come from.[11]

The *Venture Beat* article illustrates that bots are an amazing tool that allows industries to simplify their digital interfaces. Additionally, bots are easier to maintain than apps. Rather than publishing a new app to the app store for every new feature request—such as the ability to address customer questions like, "What's my credit card balance?"—the bank writes code that translates the message on the back end. Using either Facebook's chatbot or the Microsoft Bot Framework, customers can dip in and out of the e-commerce platform, performing more types of customer interactions such as payments and information requests. And in the future, technology that predicts and anticipates customer needs will be much better and more accurate overall.

Serving Customers in Their Preferred Channels

Effort is among the most important aspects of customer experience. I've said it before and I'll say it again: make your processes harder on you—the business—and easier on your customers. That means serving customers in the way they would like to be served. Of course, we can't talk about serving customers in the way they want to be served without talking about the channels via which they prefer to be served.

As I mentioned earlier, customers in their personal lives enjoy the ease of communication brought by text messaging, Snapchat, Skype, Facebook Messenger, Kik, WhatsApp, Twitter, and other networks. When it comes to business, however, most companies don't make it easy for consumers to use these tools to get in touch with them. But that's starting to change: a new report reveals that 65 percent of smartphone users worldwide have used a messaging app to talk to a company. The study analyzed the responses of almost 6,000 people from nine different nations and found that over-the-top apps such as WhatsApp and Facebook Messenger, along with SMS, have become the communication platform of choice for most users who talk to companies.[12]

Some companies are making arrangements to meet the customer where the customer is, but most have not caught on. While social media has completely changed brands' ability to engage with customers, many brands have not gotten it right. Brands largely take the same controlling approach they use with their traditional channels and apply it on social media.

What does that mean? It means that brands either use social media to redirect customers to a traditional channel, such as a call center, or they task the customer with finding the brand on social media and completing tasks on the brand's terms. Today's companies make interactions harder on the customer and easier on the brand, a problematic attitude, given the increasingly competitive business environment.

We're spending much of our day on our phones, and the bigger the phone, the more time we spend. Have you heard of a phablet? This device is a cross between a smartphone and a tablet, with a screen measuring 5.5 to 6.99 inches—we can watch TV on a device we keep right in our pockets. Time spent on phablets increased by 336 percent in 2015.[13]

The most mobile-friendly businesses today are coming out of the sharing economy. Let me paint a picture for you. In one day—on my smartphone— I ordered a handcrafted ottoman through Etsy, used TaskRabbit to arrange for an electrician to install my flat-screen TV, ordered groceries to be delivered by Instacart, booked lodging on Airbnb for an upcoming trip to Prague, and then jumped in an Uber to meet a friend downtown. I did all of these things as I watched my dog play at the dog park. The world is changing, and many of us prefer to work and do business on the go. Imagine a salesperson who meets with a prospect at Starbucks. She may not want to pull out a full-size laptop to show a customer an item or a process, but she'd probably pull out a tablet or even a phablet for a demo. These are just a few examples of the many tasks we can now do on our phones.

***

Customer experience is a critical component of a competitive business strategy. It's no secret that the way consumers engage with brands is shifting, and new technology is changing customer expectations across the board. While customer service is not synonymous with customer experience, customer service is an important piece of a competitive strategy that is gaining more resources and attention within the organization. The contact center—the place where customers literally make contact with the brand—is seen by many forward-thinking business leaders as a relationship-building tool rather than a cost center.

Customers want to do business on their terms, and you can't blame them—they have a greater ability to control elements of their lives than ever before, thanks largely to technology. The digital explosion, social media, and mobile have equipped customers to get in touch with businesses 24–7. Customers don't want to wait around for companies to figure out how to meet their needs. The sharing economy, also known as the on-demand economy, has ballooned seemingly overnight to serve customers hungry for instant connection and rapid response.

But technology doesn't just enable consumers: it enables brands to evolve their offerings as well. In the next chapter, we'll talk about how companies can leverage technology to enhance customer experience.

Notes

1. Lucinda Shen, "Amazon's Stock Just Hit a Major Milestone," *Fortune*, September 22, 2016, http://fortune.com/2016/09/22/amazon-stock-history/.
2. Adam Lovinus, "B2B E-Commerce: Shop with a Phone, Buy with a Desktop?" *Newegg Business*, July 16, 2015, https://blog.neweggbusiness.com/trends/b2b-e-commerce-shop-with-a-phone-buy-with-a-desktop/.
3. Claire Groden, "Here's How Many Americans Sleep with Their Smartphones," *Fortune*, June 29, 2015, http://fortune.com/2015/06/29/sleep-banks-smartphones/.
4. Tanya Dua, "Kik Me Some Lipstick: Sephora Bets on Messaging Apps for E-Commerce," *DigiDay*, March 31, 2016, http://digiday.com/brands/see-kik-sephora-bets-messaging-apps-e-commerce/.
5. Craig Smith, "By the Numbers: 20 Important Kik Messenger Stats," *DMR*, August 25, 2016, http://expandedramblings.com/index.php/kik-messenger-stats/.

6. *Wikipedia*, s.v. "Kik Messenger," last modified November 13, 2016, https://en.wikipedia.org/wiki/Illusory_superiority.

7. Alyson Shontell, "If You Think It's Crazy That Snapchat Might Go Public at a $40 Billion Valuation, Here's Something to Consider," *Business Insider*, November 1, 2016, www.businessinsider.com/is-snapchat-ipo-worth-investing-in-2016–10.

8. Roni Jacobson, "How Snapchat's Sponsored Lenses Became a Money-Printing Machine," *Back Channel*, October 21, 2016, https://backchannel.com/how-snapchats-sponsored-lenses-became-a-money-printing-machine-a1e45b0a82b#.mij9j4zcv.

9. Joshua Topolsky, "The End of Twitter," *New Yorker*, January 29, 2016, www.newyorker.com/tech/elements/the-end-of-twitter.

10. David Iudica (Senior Director Strategic Insights & Research, Yahoo), in discussion with the author.

11. Bijan Shahrokhi, "Here's How Facebook Messenger Will Change Banking," *Venture Beat*, June 5, 2016, http://venturebeat.com/2016/06/05/say-hello-to-messenger-banking/.

12. Andrew Meola, "Long Wait Times on the Phone with Customer Service May Be a Thing of the Past," *Business Insider*, July 1, 2016, www.businessinsider.com/long-wait-times-on-the-phone-with-customer-service-may-be-a-thing-of-the-past-2016–7.

13. Brandy Shaul, "Flurry: Time Spent on Phablets Increased 334% in 2015," *Social Times*, January 5, 2016, www.adweek.com/socialtimes/flurry-time-spent-on-phablets-increased-334-in-2015/632374.

CHAPTER 3

The Growing Role of Technology in Customer Experience

Imagine a small rural village in Sweden. It is pretty much in the middle of nowhere. There's no Instacart to bring groceries, no Postmates to deliver goods to the door. It's nighttime, and a new dad accidentally spills the only remaining bottle of baby formula on the floor as his hungry son wails. A run to the closest grocery store will take at least forty minutes, round trip. Robert Illiason was that dad, and that was the moment that the technology expert started thinking about alternatives. An IT consultant who works for Ikea's automation and data department, he realized that living in a rural area, where shops close early, puts a strain on customers. Illiason came up with the idea for Näraffär (meaning "shop nearby"), the first unmanned grocery store where customers could buy small items such as baby food at any time of night or day. The entire customer experience is automated via apps, cameras, and other easy-to-use technology. He literally built a solution, and now he is contacted by companies all over the world that want to replicate his work.

Some companies are trying out self-service technologies, but clearly those technologies are not working efficiently. The intention is good, but the execution is sloppy. Two examples of this are the self-service options at Target and Safeway; while I like these stores, they have much work to do to improve their self-service experience. Because the checkout system is not without problems, an employee stands nearby to help customers by overriding the system when the technology doesn't work. This employee is generally so busy, however, that the transaction takes much longer than it would have if the customer had gone through the regular checkout. For one thing, the way the system verifies the customer's purchase of items is flawed. For example, the system requests that you put your bag on a scale and place each item in your bag after you scan it. But sometimes you have too many items, and they don't all fit on the scale. Or sometimes it takes so long to look up an item without a barcode that you regret choosing self-service. The technology isn't perfect, and the system messes up a few too many times for it to be effortless for the customer. In this case, companies, even huge ones like Target and Safeway, released customer technology that isn't finished baking yet. It would be better to wait until the systems have improved than to release technologies that make customers' lives harder.

In contrast, some small businesses are using technology to enhance the customer experience, and the process is more efficient than it is at many larger companies. My local dentist is an example: I arrived at my dentist's office yesterday and signed in on an iPad. I filled out my customer information on the same touchscreen, and all of my signatures were digital. My doctor, too, has turned to technology to make the patient experience easier. At Kaiser via their app called My Doctor Online I can talk to my doctor on video. I can also email and send photos to the doctor. Any healthcare provider that still relies on paper needs to get moving on creating a digital customer experience for their patients. While some organizations are making customer experiences more digital, the adoption rate is slow. As some companies move toward technology and others lag behind, the difference in customer experience is palpable for the customer comparing the two experiences.

Enhancing Customer Experience With Wearable Tech

In *X: The Experience When Business Meets Design*, author Brian Solis talks about how Disney created its MagicBand—an all-in-one device that connects users with their vacation options—embedded with technology that allows customers to make purchases without a credit card or cash, get in and out of the park, review and optimize wait times, book FastPass, open their hotel room door, make dinner reservations, and receive personalized offers. Solis says, "Disney's MagicBand is a brilliant representative of experience architecture." He imagines how useful this technology would be in environments such as hospitals. "Right now," Solis says,

> the number of staff used to move people around is high. As we move into the future, trying to reduce costs, you might imagine a hospital being much more like a mall, with a greater deal of self-service. . . . Someone heads down to radiology, gets scanned, and they don't have to check back in.

Disney's MagicBand is offered precisely in the spirit of "doing more," with an eye on experience architecture.

To take that experience further: I have a Fitbit Blaze watch on my arm, and with this IoT (Internet of Things) product, I have tailored information sent to me. I can access my text messages and my workouts, and can I see that eventually I may have little need for any other device. Why wouldn't I want my wallet, my music, my phone, my watch, and my workouts all on one device?

The Apple watch allows consumers to do everything they can do on their phone, on their watch. They can text anyone through a voice activation function, listen to music, track workouts and much more.

Here's another way to think about it. One challenge for companies like Disney is that not all consumers want another gadget. The point of Disney's MagicBand is to deliver content, offers, and other forms of engagement, and the company doesn't need to be the producer of the gadget, but it can instead partner with a company like Fitbit or Apple. The amazing thing about an IoT device like a watch is that if a person is awake, it's likely on that consumer's arm. If the consumer chooses, and the company's offers are compelling enough, that company can connect with that consumer anytime. That's an unprecedented opportunity for a brand, but companies need to be careful with the way they use that ability; they don't want to turn consumers off by overdoing it. If the marketing is done well, the brand can send offers, invitations to loyalty programs, and other customer service–related content when necessary. You can imagine how helpful this would be for a grocer, a retailer, or any type of business—especially one that gets actual customers to a real location.

Robots in Our Lives

While economists and futurists speculate that technology will take jobs away from people, many customers welcome easier and more convenient ways to do business with companies. Meet the robot called Pepper, a machine being used in Pizza Huts all over Asia. Pepper provides personalized order recommendations and calorie information to customers, and allows them to pay for their order using a MasterPass wallet app or by scanning a QR code on the robot's chest.

But it doesn't stop there. You may have heard of IBM's Watson, one of the more exciting innovations in the area of artificial intelligence. Artificial intelligence is the intelligence exhibited by machines or software, as well as the name of the academic field that studies how to create computer hardware and software capable of intelligent behavior.

In IBM's New York City headquarters, I watched a demo in the Watson "room," where the IBM employee compared the way we search for research, information, and treatments for rare health ailments today (via research on paper) with the way it would be done using artificial intelligence. Today, when a sick person walks into the hospital, that patient is limited by the knowledge of the doctor treating him. But imagine every doctor having the ability to input the patient's various symptoms and cross-reference them with millions of pieces of information, data, and research from all over the world. You can imagine how helpful this would be to doctors practicing in remote parts of the world. The ability to tap into cumulative and organized knowledge could save many lives.

Artificial intelligence can also be used in a customer service capacity, where a system can solve a customer problem by cross referencing hundreds of thousands of other pieces of information. For example, Watson has pioneered innovation in fashion, medicine, and sports, and now has entered the terrain of music. The computer system evaluated five years of cultural data, taking the "emotional temperature" of each year. Additionally, Watson looked at the lyrics of the one hundred most popular songs from each week of the same five-year period to learn the emotions behind each song.[1] Then Alex Da Kid, a composer who has written for Rihanna, Eminem, and Nicki Minaj, used the data to help create a "cognitive song" called "Not Easy." It debuted at number six in the fall of 2016 on Billboard's Rock Digital Song Sales chart, which tracks the week's top-downloaded rock songs.[2]

Pepper and Watson are teaming up to explore a range of use cases, serving in roles that run the gamut from in-class teaching assistants to nursing aids. Mike Rhodin, senior vice president of IBM Watson said in a statement, "We believe when cognitive capabilities are embedded in robotics people can engage and benefit from the technology in unprecedented ways."[3]

The Internet of Things

We briefly mentioned this earlier—sister to artificial intelligence is the Internet of Things (IoT), an exciting realm of connectivity predicated on sensors embedded in appliances, vehicles, buildings, and other everyday items, allowing them to interact and exchange data. In fact, many of you reading this may look down at your wrist and see some type of wearable product. I mentioned earlier that I'm wearing my Fitbit, which tells me how many steps I've walked as well as my heart rate. It sends this data back to my computer, and I can track my progress week over week. This fitness tracker is but one example of the connectivity that awaits us as the IoT ramps up, and at a not-too-distant point in the future, anything with an on or off switch will be part of the IoT family. Information from our products will be sent to our phone and to our computer, and vice versa. Data about our behavior will be sent directly from the products we use to the companies we purchase from, and the companies we purchase from will send us content directly through the products we buy.

IoT will completely change the way consumers interact with their products. According to a study released by Cisco, the number of connected devices is projected to top *75 billion* by 2020, and a recent McKinsey report pegs the economic impact of IoT applications at *$11.1 trillion annually* by 2025.[4] Companies are sprinting to get a piece of the space, as it's an industry on a huge growth trajectory. In 2015, Salesforce released an IoT Cloud that aims to process huge amounts of device data and help businesses build customer profiles, take actions, and respond directly to customers based on IoT events.[5]

An article on TechTarget summed up the power of IoT when it comes to customer experience: while brands currently have the opportunity to connect with consumers via methods other than a warranty card, IoT provides an even greater opportunity to immediately connect to the user via an IoT product that's always on. As we highlighted in the last section, smart products that customers actually wear provides a great opportunity to engage that customer. When I wear my Fitbit watch, for example, Fitbit can send me a message anytime via the display. If I am awake, I am wearing it. Not only will IoT provide easier and better ways for companies to interact with customers, but the company can leverage IoT to capture data and help companies better understand the behavior of their customers. Think about the many ways that companies can create unlimited personalized interactions with customers via IoT products, and about how they can leverage analytics in smarter ways and change the way they engage with customers overall. IoT will allow companies to know their customers better so they can tailor content and preferences in real time.

Products That Listen, Analyze, and Talk

Increasingly, our products will be able to fix themselves by accessing software. We're all familiar with the idea of a product recall: a company sells a customer a product, and the product is later deemed unsafe or unreliable by a consumer affairs department. The company realizes it must tell millions of customers that they need to return the product. As more and more of our products are connected to technology, companies will have greater opportunity to fix product issues remotely.

In the future, products will be able to identify and diagnose their own problems, and fix those problems without a lot of customer intervention.

Just as your iPhone updates itself every so often, your products, as they become smarter, will be able to fix themselves. Cars from Tesla Motors are perhaps our closest example of a self-diagnosing and self-repair product. Tesla cars run on software. When the car needs to be fixed, you can update the software from your phone.

According to Tesla's website, the latest software update improves the user interface:

> Software update 8.0 kicks off a significant over-the-air overhaul of the Tesla touchscreen and introduces the biggest UI revamp since the launch of Model S . . . 8.0 combines a modern look with updates to Autopilot, Navigation with Trip Planner, Maps, and the Media Player for a safer, more advanced driving experience.[6]

Tesla figured out what customers wanted and built one of the more elegant user interfaces on the car. It simply looked at what customers dislike about the driving experience, and set about to improve it—with little effort for the customer. In the future, more and more of our products will self-diagnose and fix themselves while we work, play, or sleep.

While in the past technology has arguably made the customer experience worse, in the future, technology will make the customer experience better. One recent example comes from Absolut, which is working on a smart bottle that will add value to the consumer in real time. If purchased at an airport, for example the Absolut smart bottle might offer a complimentary lunch at a private club at that same airport. The company also sees an opportunity for the smart bottle's technology to help customers who are partying get safe rides home.

And adults aren't the only beneficiaries of IoT products. Hello Barbie is a connected doll from Mattel that has the ability to listen, understand, and respond to customers. I watched a Mattel demo conference, during which the woman demoing Hello Barbie said,

> She's the first doll that can engage in learning. She plays games, tells jokes, inspires storytelling—and she even listens to the girl's [assuming

the consumer would be a girl] preferences and adapts to those. She has Wi-Fi capability stored in the cloud and we can push data to her.

In the Mattel sales representative's demo, which you can find on YouTube, she talked to Hello Barbie and said, "Hey [Barbie], look, we're on stage!"[7] Barbie responded, "It's very exciting to be on stage." The woman doing the demo agreed. Later, the woman from Mattel asked Barbie's advice regarding what she should be when she grows up. Barbie—remembering their previous conversation—responded, "Since you like being on stage, maybe a dancer or a politician?" Barbie demonstrated her ability to listen and use the information she collected in future communications. Some see possibilities for this doll to help with interactive learning and monitor health issues.

Another example that demonstrates the potential of the IoT comes from Altiux, a product engineering, design, and technology firm services company for the connected world. Have you ever looked out the window of an airplane that's landing at night? You see thousands of lights glimmering along the city skyline. You might wonder how many of those lights are truly necessary. What if more than half of them don't need to be on at all? It's a very wasteful use of energy. Altiux aimed to solve the problem of waste by helping to create "smart cities," and part of its portfolio is a product that addresses parking and parking lots, in essence making them smart. This technology can help lower costs and save energy by determining in real time what areas need to be illuminated. Can you imagine if we used this type of technology all over our cities? We would save a great deal of energy and other resources if we were to make more of our cities "smart."

The Nest Learning Thermostat aspires to bring smart energy management to interior spaces with an electronic, programmable, and self-learning Wi-Fi-enabled thermostat that optimizes heating and cooling of homes and businesses to conserve energy. It is based on a machine-learning algorithm: For the first few weeks, users have to regulate the thermostat in order to provide a reference dataset. Nest can then learn people's schedules, the temperatures they prefer, and when those settings should be used. Built-in sensors and geolocation data provided by smartphones tell the device to shift the system into energy-saving mode when nobody is home.[8] Can you imagine if we employed such devices on a vast scale? If every home, car, boat, and machine had a self-learning aspect, we would greatly decrease our energy waste. We are not very far away from self-regulating products like these. Another exciting new development comes from Amazon who now offers customers a complimentary visit from a Smart Home consultant who will come to your house to educate you about how to make your house "smart." In fact we had a Smart Home consultant come to our house and teach us about how to use a self-regulating thermostat, voice activated lights and television. The smart home offerings are linked to the voice activated device Alexa Echo. If a device can be linked to the Amazon Echo it can be controlled, and monitored by this operating system. Alexa acts as the central operating system of the house running all of your programs and applications. Anything with an on or off switch has the potential to be controlled by Alexa in the future.

How the On-Demand Economy Is Changing Customer Experience

People seek flexibility in their personal lives, they seek flexibility at work, and now they seek flexibility from the companies they do business with. Let's face it, customers want products and services when they want them, and if you're not able to cater to that desire, you might find your company out of business.

Think about it from the customer's perspective. Life happens, and customers need services without much notice. For example, we have a newborn at home, and we also have two Yorkie rescues that have a lot of energy. When my husband is away, it's much harder to walk the dogs, but I can easily book a dog walker through the on-demand company Rover, managing the entire transaction via the app. The app provides reviews of the dog walkers, notifies the owner when the dog walker has left with the dogs for the walk, and even asks the dog walker to submit photos of the dog on the walk. This amazing service allows me to get help without much notice. The on-demand economy has ballooned because of its convenience, competitive pricing, and fulfillment of customer needs that haven't been met yet. Customers want businesses that will meet them when and where they want to be met.

In her 2015 Internet Trends report, Mary Meeker highlighted various "just-in-time" companies operating mainly in the sharing economy. There is clearly growing interest in on-demand companies of all kinds, and Mary Meeker cites a few reasons that on-demand services have taken off in the past few years. These include "smartphone adoption, mobile payment platforms and social authentication." Another reason is that the on-demand style of work suits millennials. The same report argues that changes in connectivity and commerce impact the ways people can work, but it's still early in the game. There are now on-demand services for virtually every category, from makeup and hair (e.g., Vensette, Madison Reed, and Style Bee) to massage (e.g., Zeel). Companies are making it easier than ever to get services that were once only offered to customers who visited a salon, spa, or other such location; now, the service comes directly to you.

I like examples from the sharing economy because the activity is new enough that the involved businesses take customer experience very seriously. If you have a problem as a customer, you report it easily through techno-logical means, and it is fixed right away. I have never had to contact a call center for any company in the sharing economy I've ever done business with. Technology makes the advertising, marketing, booking, customer service, and feedback process simple. This is precisely what *More Is More* is about— working hard on customer experience so transactions and interactions are easy and almost mindless for the customer.

Think about how the world is changing—today, the world's largest taxi company owns no taxis (Uber), the largest accommodations provider owns no real estate (Airbnb), the most popular media owner creates no content (Facebook), the largest telecom operators own no telecom infrastructure (Skype and WeChat), the world's largest software vendors don't write the apps (Apple and Google), and the world's largest movie house owns no cin-emas (Netflix).[9] The world is changing rapidly, and brands that aren't char-acterized as part of the on-demand or sharing economies are now competing with the expectations set by brands operating within those new economies. In the next section, we look at all the major trends affecting customer experience and what you need to be aware of.

Airbnb Case Study: Elegant Digital and Mobile Experiences Delivered

No one would have thought, ten years ago, that there would be a new service model that facilitated people's stays in the homes of total strangers—and that this would make a sizable dent in the enormous hospitality industry. But it happened. Airbnb offers easy user experiences, an important piece of customer experience. Not only is service strong, but the company has clearly walked through the customer journey and considered every move the customer might make. The customers never have to think about user experience because it's set up to be mindless for them.

Customers should not even realize they are on a customer journey—all they should know is how easy it is to do what they want to do, such as search for destinations or book a rental. On the Airbnb site, there's are properties available at a range of prices, allowing people who previously couldn't afford to travel to easily book a room. When I open the app, it's clean and beautiful, like a magazine. I am greeted with a personal message: "Hi, Blake. Where to next?" I can browse my recent searches, get ideas "just for the weekend," check out Airbnb favorites, review popular destinations, or read a number of guidebooks for cities I might be interested in visiting. I can easily review past trips or my communication history with my past hosts. Customer service and payments are easy. I receive a text notification that takes me directly to Airbnb in-app messaging with my host, and I can text my host when I arrive. One particular trip to Philadelphia was memorable. I never met the host because I didn't have to. He provided amazing self-service, and it wasn't necessary for him to be there in person. The key to the apartment was secured in a keypad for which I was given the code. The host had printed out a list of places to go, things to see, and restaurants to try. He had stocked the fridge with healthy snacks. He'd thought of everything. I gave him a perfect review, adding to the many top-star reviews he'd received before mine.

Airbnb represents the pinnacle of modern customer experience. The company facilitates incredible experiences with a seamless customer journey via its technology, and it practices what it preaches. Brian Chesky, CEO and cofounder of Airbnb, is himself a host, meaning that he offers up his own apartment for Airbnb customers to rent. Everything about the interactions between hosts and customers is human. The company's motto is, "Don't go there. Live there." Airbnb features larger-than-life videos on their homepage depicting happy customers enjoying breakfast in an ethereal nook in an exotic location.

***

Mobile must not be the afterthought of your digital experience. Instead, it must be a core piece of your digital strategy. And that digital strategy needs to simply be better than that of your competitors. It must be thoughtful and must consider the life your customer is living: How will you leverage digital to make your customers' lives easier and better? In the next chapter, we'll look at how big data should also make customers' lives easier, and how your brand can set out to do that.

Notes

1. IBM, "How IBM Watson Inspired Alex Da Kid's New Song 'Not Easy,'" *Business Insider*, October 25, 2016, www.businessinsider.com/sc/ibm-watson-helps-create-alex-da-kid-song-2016-10.
2. Gary Trust, "Alex Da Kid Hits Rock Charts with Watson BEAT Collab 'Not Easy,'" *Billboard*, March 11, 2016, www.billboard.com/articles/columns/chart-beat/7565454/alex-da-kid-rock-charts-watson-beat-not-easy.
3. Darryl Taft, "IBM's Rometty Takes Watson to CES," *Declara*, January 6, 2016, https://declara.com/content/A5YOqw21.
4. Syed Zaeem Hosain, "Reality Check: 50B IoT Devices Connected by 2020: Beyond the Hype and into Reality," *RSR Wirless News*, June 28, 2016, www.rcrwireless.com/20160628/opinion/reality-check-50b-iot-devices-connected-2020-beyond-hype-reality-tag10.

5. Ginny Marvin, "Salesforce Gets into Internet of Things Market with IoT Cloud," *Marketing Land*, September 15, 2015, http://marketingland.com/salesforce-gets-into-internet-of-things-market-with-iot-cloud-142684.

6. Lambert Fred, "Tesla v8.0 Software Update Is Being Pushed Right Now, All the Details and Full Release Notes," *Electrek*, September 22, 2016, https://electrek.co/2016/09/22/tesla-v8–0-software-update-is-being-pushed-right-now-all-the-details-and-full-release-notes/.

7. Chip Chick, "Hello Barbie Is The World's First Interactive Barbie Doll," February 15, 2015, www.youtube.com/watch?v=RJMvmVCwoNM.

8. *Wikipedia*, s.v. "Nest Labs," last modified November 16, 2016, https://en.wikipedia.org/wiki/Nest_Labs.

9. Susan Visser, "5 Disruptive Technologies That Are Challenging the Traditional Banking Model," *IBM Big Data and Analytics Hub*, May 16, 2016, www.ibmbigdatahub.com/blog/5-disruptive-technologies-are-challenging-traditional-banking-model.

CHAPTER 4

Cleaning Up a Mess of Big Data and Marketing

Perhaps you've heard of comedian Tig Notaro. Notaro became famous when she did a stand-up comedy routine about a harrowing few months she'd had. Her first lines were, "Hello. I have cancer." Not only had she gotten cancer, she caught a deadly bacterial infection, lost twenty-five pounds, got pneumonia, had to undergo a double mastectomy, was dumped by her partner who didn't want to deal with the cancer, and, to make matters much worse, her mom suddenly fell, hit her head, and died in a hospital. While none of this was funny, Notaro's delivery that night on stage moved people. The comedian Louis CK happened to be in the crowd and called her stand-up performance one of the best he'd ever witnessed. It made waves throughout the Internet and made her famous.

So, what does Tig Notaro have to do with customer experience? What I'm about to tell you is exactly what is wrong with customer experience across most companies: processes are created with no thought for the actual customer. Here's one example: a hospital sent Notaro's deceased mother a questionnaire in the mail. It was a survey about how her recent stay was. You read that right. The hospital sent a dead woman a survey about her recent stay.

You just can't make these stories up—and they happen all the time. But how do they happen? Usually, such disconnects occur because companies seek to process customers faster and faster without stopping to consider whether the practices make sense. How much irrelevant snail mail and e-mail do most people get? A lot. How often are ads actually relevant to individual customers? Not that often! How often do customers get multiple e-mails from the same company? Even worse is the tendency of a company's marketing team to auto-add e-mails to its newsletter roster. Or trick customers into signing up for a newsletter. I don't know about you, but when I get an e-mailed newsletter from a company that did this, I'm very turned off. Companies are in such a rush to capture customer information that they don't stop to consider whether customers even need or want content from them. Every day, companies are committing atrocities against customers in the form of poor experiences. The customer data they have could be used to provide relevant messaging, but companies today are still creating mass experiences. And that is how a hospital sends a customer feedback survey to a dead woman.

Data Security

Because of the proliferation of security breaches, which seem to occur every week now, many of us get e-mails prompting us to change our passwords. You may have heard of Ashley Madison, an online dating service, with 39 million members in fifty-three countries, marketed to people who are married or in relationships. A data security breach at Ashley Madison revealed that some customers thought they had deleted their data, but that customer data had not been removed. Because of the site's policy of not deleting users' personal information—including real names, home addresses, search history, and credit card transaction records—many users feared being publicly shamed. The company then required those who had profiles on the website—some of which had been made by others as pranks—pay to remove them.[1] The data these users paid $19 to have removed was never actually deleted. When the company was hacked their information was exposed.

Another famous data breach comes from Sony. Almost a year before the Ashley Madison hack, a group released confidential data from Sony Pictures Entertainment that included personal information about Sony Pictures employees and their families, e-mails between employees, and information about salaries. A group demanded that Sony pull its film *The Interview*, a comedy about a plot to assassinate North Korean leader Kim Jong-un, and threatened to attack any movie theater screening the movie. In response, movie houses chose not to screen the film, and Sony sent the movie straight to digital release with a limited theatrical release the next day. U.S. officials believed North Korea was responsible for the hack.[2]

The Sony example represents every company's worst nightmare. Every CIO today is concerned with data security as hackers become increasingly sophisticated in their ability to break into even the most seemingly secure systems. In 2016, Mary Meeker, author of the Internet Trends report, said, "The proliferation of data generated by a multitude of devices has fostered tremendous business opportunity, but privacy concerns abound."[3]

A Software-Defined Society

Robert Tercek, former president of digital media for the Oprah Winfrey Network and the author of *Vaporized: Solid Strategies for Success in a Dematerialized World*, believes that we are living in a "software-defined society," in which we are subject to a world programmed by software companies. According to Tercek, we spend more than ten hours a day looking at a digital screen, and the companies that track our behavior know more about our own behavior than we do. There will undoubtedly be increasing debate about how software systems can create challenges for laws, civic norms, and regulations, including basic citizens' rights, such as privacy. Part of that debate will be the government's proper role in protecting its citizens' data. For example, can a social network sell your data to an advertiser?

Recently, the FBI asked Apple to create a backdoor to the iPhone, an unprecedented request from a government agency. The FBI made its request in order to get into a phone to collect information related to a terrorism case. Everyone on the Internet had an opinion on this issue. Was Apple protecting its customers or acting against the government in an unpatriotic way? It soon became clear that Apple felt that, by creating a backdoor to the iPhone, it might unwittingly provide access to others through the backdoor as well. Tercek remarked, "Apple's commitment to its customers puts them at odds with their own government. Software is starting to confront the real world. There will one day be a collision and we'll see this more frequently."

Today, the government, particularly in the United States, is not heavily involved in discussions around technology and data. Decisions regarding the collection of data and the tracking of consumer behavior are shaped largely by the companies that seek to make money from the data. Tercek believes that advertisers are still making most of the decisions regarding data, such as which data is tracked. He said, "These are arbitrary business decisions made by the people who are out to maximize their earnings—they're not too concerned with customers. We'll see this emerge in different ways as we spend more of our time in digital networks." Tercek believes that the debates about data and privacy are healthy, and that we in the United States don't talk about data and privacy as much as those living in Europe do. The reason? Europe, he says, has survived Communism and surveillance societies, where people lived in fear every day.

> If you go to Europe, you'll see this is on the front page of the newspaper every day. This includes the right to privacy, who owns my data, who owns my search behavior, who can control if I appear in search results or not.

Tercek advocates for greater awareness about data privacy because, Tercek argues, in the United States, we are "clueless about the issue."

Others agree that consumers are generally blind to issues surrounding data protection. An explosive documentary, *Terms and Conditions May Apply* by Cullen Hoback, discloses the risks people face when they automatically agree to the terms of service and privacy policies of companies like Facebook, Google, and LinkedIn. The truth is that most consumers never read the terms and conditions. Is a company responsible for educating its customers about what they're signing, and, if so, to what extent is it responsible? Should legal continue to create long, wordy documents with text that is difficult for the average user to understand? If you really care about your customers, put yourself in their shoes. Do you want to read 3,000 words before you agree to terms and conditions, so you can proceed with the task you're trying to complete? Probably not! Consider putting the communication into easy-to-understand language. What are the most important things the customer needs to understand?

While it's important to protect your company, it's also important to protect your customer. Don't be afraid to do something creative with your terms and conditions—if you're trying to educate your customer, you can even use animated storytelling in marketing. Your customers will appreciate your transparency as well as your commitment to their education. I realize that if you're in the legal department, you are probably thinking, "We would never do that!" But think about how refreshing it is when a company gives you the plain truth rather than overwhelming you with fine print. It's in your interest as a company to be transparent with your customers and to help them avoid making mistakes they will later regret.

Getting the Most Out of Your Data

Good data management has benefits for customers downstream. As the company gets bigger, these areas become more important. Poor security is one of those things that can spell disaster even for a start-up—if someone hacks your website, your company could very well be finished. A good database will help you feed data insights back into your product, improving its quality. Every company has data on its customers, but the quality of that data varies from company to company. Most companies have flaws in their data that need to be corrected. Address information may be incorrect or incomplete if a customer makes a mistake while filling in her zip code, for example; sometimes, software can automatically fix the data for the company. Every company out there knows the value of clean and consistent data, but it may not come in clean. It must go through a data-cleansing process. The company must rid the data of imperfections so it's usable.

Machine Learning Helps Companies Make Decisions

Have you ever watched the HBO TV show *Westworld*? The show explores themes of consciousness in robots. Just as the robots on the show gained the ability to listen and interpret their human counterparts, our technologies will improve in their ability to listen and interpret customer behavior, with the help of machine learning. In the past a human's work was preferable to a machine's work because it was more accurate. A human could review all angles and make an educated decision. However with advances technology, many believe machine work will soon be preferable to a human's. Machine learning is a kind of artificial intelligence that provides computers the ability to learn without being programmed to do so.[4] This is the challenge we have with artificial intelligence: often, the tools don't listen effectively and can't make decisions based on the information given. This is one of the problems machine learning aims to solve today. Machine learning's uses are vast and varied.

Amazon Go provides one example of a modern application of machine learning. This new grocery store has no lines and no checkout. Using machine learning and a mix of other technologies, Amazon Go has designed a store at which customers can easily shop and then simply leave the store with the products they've chosen. A customer scans her phone upon entering the store, and then can shop without any follow-up transaction needed.

Machine learning is employed in Google's self-driving cars, in recommendations provided on Amazon and Netflix, and in fraud-detection systems. Machine learning also helps companies provide relevant contextual information to customers.

Through machine learning, you, as a company, can gain unique access to information about your customers in order to personalize their experience. Through the cloud, systems can gain access to datasets, including social media analytics. In this case, the cloud and machine learning systems work together to aggregate vast amounts of data and provide predictive analysis as well as other insightful information.

A real-life example comes from Microsoft customer Real Madrid (the Spanish soccer team), which uses machine learning to analyze the superfans who visit the team's website or connect on social media. Real Madrid's marketing team uses machine learning to cut up those data and provide tailored content. For example, some fans, rather than showing interest in the entire team, prefer information about one player. Machine learning helps filter content to provide information about player news, uniforms, and appearances. Not all fans can get to a game but, using machine learning, Real Madrid can give fans information on how to watch games online. Fans also get recommendations for products based on what team gear they've recently purchased. Fans who have never been to a game get information on how to watch the games online and receive product recommendations based on the team gear they have purchased previously. To meet individual needs and provide personal experiences, Real Madrid breaks their fans into micro-markets. Machine learning can be a hugely powerful tool for brands.

Are Personas Useful?

We can't talk about customer data without considering personas. Many companies, including some at which I've worked, are very focused on customer personas. I always found it strange that we would depict our customers as cute mock-ups of humans, either illustrated or with stock photos. Particularly when customer bases are dynamic, always fluid-changing. Personas are generally used to guide marketing decisions for products or services. According to UX Magazine,

> A persona represents a cluster of users who exhibit similar behavioral patterns in their purchasing decisions, use of technology or products, customer service preferences, lifestyle choices, and the like. Behaviors, attitudes, and motivations are common to a 'type' regardless of age, gender, education, and other typical demographics.[5]

Creating personas may be a very popular exercise in marketing, but how accurate and useful are they? Siddharth Gaikwad, former global head of digital and customer experience for Dell Business Services had the same question, and he spoke with me about personas for this book. Gaikwad believes that with 100 new domain registrations and more than 600 websites created every minute, plus 20,000 apps submitted via the Apple App Store every month, "We can almost be certain that every potential customer or user must be interacting with at least a couple of those and generating meaningful data" (Gaikwad, personal communication).

Let's think for a second about the vast amount of data being created. Consumers using web and mobile touch points are creating close to 3 quintillion bytes of data every single day, Gaikwad points out. He notes that's the equivalent of 2.5 million hard disks of one terabyte each. Users on publishing platforms like WordPress add more than 1 million web pages every day. Twitter is a conduit for 500 million tweets a day—that's like 12,000 copies of *Harry Potter and the Order of the Phoenix*, the longest book in the series.[6]

Gaikwad wrote to me in an e-mail, "Do you think we have the time or the need to sit back and make user personas in a world where the same users are generating quintillion bytes of data every single day? In most cases, I believe not!" He went on to say:

Personas were relevant in the past, but not in this digital age, where data is omnipresent, rich, and real time. It's no more about knowing the user or usage patterns through personas. It is about knowing where the user data lies and how to make sense of it. The term "persona" has a few new labels, thanks to big data and advanced analytics. Some call it "propensity to buy or use," some call it "next best action," and some "single score"! These are new methods used to arrive at business and design decisions. These new methods don't [need to] rely on traditional processes such as interviews and focus group sessions because of the fact that data needed to derive insights is already there.

So, will we make educated guesses from made-up personas? Or do we look directly at what the data are telling us in real time?

Gaikwad added:

"Propensity to buy" is a predictive model that predicts which customers are ready to buy and when. This is a powerful tool for sales makers. Similarly, "Next best action," again a predictive model, analyses historical data so that businesses can offer personalized services based on the customer's behavioral patterns and context. This is a powerful tool for customer service contact center employees. There are many predictive models such as these above that help in deriving engagement, psychographic, physiological, and consumption patterns to serve consumers when, where, and in the manner which they desire. Thanks to digital technologies, the term "personas" has a new definition and new design processes associated with it that businesses can use to buy, sell, or service opportunities. We may still need to use traditional methods such as interviews and focus groups in certain cases where technology adoption is nascent—like health care in emerging markets. However, for most businesses where technology is not nascent, the new definitions and processes are paramount!

In other words, we now have more data than we have had at any point in history, and we also have more feedback than we've ever had—so why are we fixated on made-up personas? I'm skeptical that personas are helpful and prefer to stick to the facts.

When Marketers Are in the Wrong Place at the Wrong Time

Yesterday, my husband and I were driving one of our two dogs to the emergency room. My husband, Jacob, was driving, and I was navigating with Waze, one of the all-time most popular GPS apps. As we got on the freeway, I noticed a large red banner ad across my phone. At first glance I thought this was a cautionary announcement about the road; for example, Waze will tell you when there's something dangerous on the shoulder of the road, if there's a shorter route, or if there's a delay on your route. However, the banner wasn't making any of these announcements; instead, it was an ad notifying me that there was a McDonald's restaurant on my drive to the ER, with an image advertising soda and sweet tea for $1. The ad also said it would add three minutes to my route. If I swiped right on the banner, the GPS on Waze would direct me to McDonald's. First, I don't eat McDonald's; Waze goofed by assuming the product it is advertising is even of interest to its customers. Second, it's dangerous to put a banner across a phone when the user is employing GPS. If I were the one driving and this red banner on my phone caught my eye, I might think it was an emergency. It could distract me from driving or confuse me into making a wrong turn. However, Waze doesn't appear to be discerning in its advertising strategy. McDonald's might be pleased to try this "just in time" advertising tactic, as consumers are less interested in billboards along the freeway, but this tactic is simply another example of mass messaging, interruptive, ill timed, and irrelevant.

Many Marketers Rely on "the Insertion" Approach

Most marketers still embrace a strategy of "insertion." For many years, marketers and advertisers have relied on their ability to insert themselves into consumers' favorite content. However, consumers today are happy to pay for content that is completely free of advertising. It's the HBO model applied across multiple channels, not just television.

Brands still rely on mass advertising via broadcast platforms like television, but the world is changing. Programming without traditional advertising is gaining ground—Netflix is now home to some of the most beloved shows in the world. While it's not always easy to get consumers to pay for premium content, they will shell out good money if the content adds enough value to their lives. Consumers have had a taste of how good entertainment is when it's not interrupted by advertising, and many people now won't watch live shows—they record shows and skip through the commercials. Consumers are learning how nice life is without disruptions from marketers that insert themselves. And it's not just the television industry that will be upended in the next few years—the publishing industry, too, is facing massive disruption. All around us, the world of content is changing. If consumers enjoy TV uninterrupted by ads, they wonder why they can't have the same customer experience on other communication channels. Publishers and brands will need to find new ways to engage customers, focusing more on providing value and less on broadcasting advertisements. And the challenge for advertisers extends beyond traditional media like television and online magazines to social media.

Recent statistics should alarm marketers. In a *Fortune* magazine online article titled, "Brands Are Using Social Media More Than Ever, and Users Are Ignoring Them More Than Ever,"[7] writer Erin Griffith details the shocking dip in social media engagement. In 2014, Instagram posts from brands created interactions with 4.2 percent of a brand's followers. In 2015, that fell to 2.2 percent. On Pinterest, interactions fell from 0.1 percent to 0.04 percent. According to Griffith, consumers are developing "banner blindness." While many of us in our own lives prefer the idea of permission-based marketing, when it comes to what we do at work we are still relying on insertion. But insertion is becoming harder and harder. The proliferation of content on the web is making it increasingly challenging to make messages land.

There's an ongoing battle between consumers and marketers: marketers do whatever they can to insert their messages in front of consumers, and consumers do whatever they can to avoid having to watch, listen to, or read marketers' messages. If such marketers were embodied in a person at a party, this person would be chasing guests around and talking *at* them. At some point, that person is simply not going to be invited to parties. Consumers will find gatherings that don't have marketers at them. My assessment may sound harsh, but think about the situation from the perspective of the customer. Would you want to be constantly interrupted or even brainwashed by products and services that aren't relevant? I certainly don't.

Personalization is the only way marketers will get a key that lets them into the life of the consumer. Social networks and publishers have to find a balance, providing value to consumers, while also finding ways to make money. Social media users want to use these networks for free, but nothing is free. Users provide their personal data, and social networks find ways to make money by giving brands the opportunity to engage with consumers on the platform. The youth of today—generation Z—have enjoyed more control over their content than any generation in history. The way marketers will earn entree into customer conversations is by creating compelling products. In providing value in the form of utility, they will earn access into their customers' lives.

***

In today's digital era, you cannot not treat all your customers the same. Avoid sending customers irrelevant messaging, be smart about how you talk about your customers internally (are personas really the answer?), and when you reach out to customers, ensure that you're adding value to their lives. Care about your customers' data even if they don't require you to. You want your brand to have a reputation as an upstanding organization—not a sleazy money machine that tricks customers into giving away their data. Finally, if you're not adding value, don't insert your message into your customers' view.

Notes

1. *Wikipedia*, s.v. "Ashley Madison," last modified November 16, 2016, https://en.wikipedia.org/wiki/Ashley_Madison.
2. *Wikipedia*, s.v. "Sony Pictures Entertainment Hack," last modified November 19, 2016, https://en.wikipedia.org/wiki/Sony_Pictures_Entertainment_hack.
3. Mary Meeker, "Internet Trends 2016," *KPCB*, June 1, 2016, www.kpcb.com/blog/2016-internet-trends-report.
4. "Definition: Machine Learning," *WhatIs.com*, http://whatis.techtarget.com/definition/machine-learning.
5. Kevin O'Connor, "Personas: The Foundation of a Great User Experience," *UX Magazine*, March 25, 2011, https://uxmag.com/articles/personas-the-foundation-of-a-great-user-experience.

6. Bharat, "How Much Data Do We Generate Every Day," *Digital Callout*, November 21, 2015, www.digitalcallout.com/2015/12/how-much-data-do-we-generate-every-day.html?m=1.

7. Erin Griffith, "Brands Are Using Social Media More Than Ever, and Users Are Ignoring Them More Than Ever," *Fortune*, August 25, 2016, http://fortune.com/2015/08/25/social-media-brands-ignore/.

PART 2

Creating Knock-Your-Socks-Off Customer Experience

D.O.M.O.R.E.

In the beginning of the book, I talked about why more is more. More means designing elegant mobile and digital experiences. As authors Ben Reason, Lavrans Løvlie, and Melvin Brand Flu discuss in *Service Design for Business: A Practical Guide to Optimizing Experience*, there's a natural friction between the business and the customer. Typically, the business is working to service and scale its customer operation, focusing on standardizing processes and driving efficiency. That means companies want to push large numbers of customers through processes that are as efficient as possible. They'd rather not have to deal with unique customer requests or variation. The idea is to make a profit while spending as little company time and money as is practicable.

Here's the point of friction: customers are individuals, and they want their specific needs met. The organization is built to manage demand, and the more the company relies on operational efficiencies to manage those demands, the more impersonal and mechanical the experience feels. Unfortunately, impersonal and mechanical customer experiences are real mood killers when it comes to building relationships.

While companies might think customers don't know much about what happens inside company walls, in truth, the customer can learn everything she wants to know about the company's functionality—or lack thereof—from the customer experience. *Service Design for Business* captures the idea that there's a tension that occurs when customers are passed from one department to another or, worse, lost in the transfer. Rather than building an experience that is based on the customer's journey, companies base the experience on what is simplest and most cost effective for the company. The company controls the experience and plans it around the organization's preferred method of moving the customer through the funnel. The companies that "D.O.M.O.R.E." go above and beyond; they focus on the customer as they build their products and services, and they take into account the ways in which customers interact with those products and services. Waiting until the end of the customer journey and addressing customers only through damage control is a mistake—and it's one far too many companies make. This is as opposed to doing it at the end in the form of damage control. Your product or service has likely already been replicated. So, what are you doing to stand out?

CHAPTER 5

Design Something Special

You can't build a compelling customer experience around a mediocre product or service. Even if your product or service isn't unique, it has to be good. You have to deliver it in a way that makes customers think, "Wow!" While Amazon products can be found on other websites, the digital experience is unparalleled, and that experience, matched with the company's customer promise—customers trust Amazon—makes it the best in the industry. Originally, Amazon CEO Jeff Bezos couldn't figure out how to grow Amazon.com organically to provide the diverse product portfolio he imagined, so he focused on the third-party marketplace (I talk more about this shift in strategy later in the chapter.[1] Once your company figures out how to meet an unmet customer need, you still must deliver that experience in a memorable way—memorable because it made the customer's life easier or better.

Surf Air Case Study: Making an Un-Fun Industry Elegant and Easy

Let's learn from an innovative company out of the sharing economy. As a general rule, flying today is terrible. But Surf Air aims to change that perception. A California-based membership airline, Surf Air offers first-class travel on what it calls executive aircraft. CEO Jeff Potter is on a mission to bring private air travel to people who thought they'd never be able to fly on a private plane. With the current global state of air travel, the timing for an Uber of the sky is better than good. Although Surf Air is still fairly small in scale, the potential is there for Surf Air or a similar provider to compete directly with the large airlines.

CEO Jeff Potter understands the value of his offering—he is saving his customers their most valuable asset: time. When I spoke with Potter, he told me that Surf Air saves its customers two to three hours every time they fly. Most travelers spend much more time getting to the airport and dealing with delays and traffic in the airport security line than they do actually sitting on an airplane. In May 2016, American Airlines reported that 70,000 of its passengers missed their flights due to excessive wait times. Additionally, 40,000 checked bags were delayed in TSA screenings and did not travel on their scheduled flight.[2] And year after year, airlines take away more of the comforts that travelers once enjoyed on flights. Surf Air conducts extensive background checks on all passengers and looks weekly at the no-fly list. Because of this regular review and the membership nature of the business, customers save a lot of time checking in and out of security. Eighty-five percent of Surf Air's customers are travelling for business, and the ease with which they can get a flight is a big appeal. Travelers can book a flight on their phone with little notice.

CEO Jeff Potter says, "We are providing a private aviation experience at current airline prices." He describes the experience as white glove:

> You pull up to a private terminal, you have a parking valet who takes your car—you walk inside this terminal and you check in with a concierge who greets you by name. Our pilots live near the terminal where they fly out of and return home to at the end of the day. As a result, the pilots see the same customers consistently and build relationships with those customers.

Potter continues, "When we interview pilots, we ensure they meet our employment requirements but we also spend half a day with them on the culture side. We want to make sure they're comfortable interacting with members."

When you arrive at your destination, you are met by a concierge, who asks if you need a rental car or an Uber, or if you have any other needs. Your luggage is brought to you within a few minutes. Surf Air seeks to remove the ordinary stresses, aggravations, and time sucks that travelers ordinarily face, drawing customers who travel frequently, can afford luxury, and are willing to pay for an above-par experience.

Take a lesson from Surf Air, and

- Think about all the terrible practices in your industry, and aim to make those terrible aspects easier for your customers.
- Start small, with a manageable number of new products or experiences, and grow from there.
- Consider all the reasons customers seek to do business with you rather than your competitors and leverage them (for example, Surf Air's customers also enjoy the exclusivity of flying among peers—they generate new business by networking during the flights).

Shoes of Prey Case Study: Creations Tailored to Customers' Tastes

Companies offering white glove service are not the only ones ratcheting up the customer experience game—companies that provide personalized experiences are doing the same. Shoes of Prey, a website where you can create and order your own shoes online, provides a completely tailored on-demand experience. While the customer has the ability to go into a store like Nordstrom to touch samples of Shoes of Prey products, customers conduct most of their interaction via the web.

If we step back and look at the trend toward on-demand products, we realize that we are just scratching the surface of the on-demand economy. Today's customers want just-in-time experiences, and interest in on-demand offerings is skyrocketing. Traditional retail stores stock millions of items, and they have no idea whether those products will sell. If companies can figure out the supply chain logistics of offering on-demand products, they will be able to act in the best interests of their customers as well as their business. The customer gets something completely tailored to her unique needs; the company no longer loses money on overstocked inventory.

Many retail stores have dysfunctional inventory processes. If a woman walks into a dress shop and the store doesn't have her size or preferred color, she's going to walk out with nothing. However, if she can effortlessly order the dress she wants in a fabric, color, and size that meet her needs, the company will not lose her business due to lack of inventory. Shoes of Prey was a start-up that broke even in two months and had multimillion-dollar revenue in less than two years. I interviewed Jodie Fox, Shoes of Prey cofounder, who said:

> Richard Branson put forth the idea of wealth and luxury—it's not about what you have but the experiences [you have]. On Instagram you might recoil if you see someone with an expensive item, but if you see them doing something extraordinary you will be impressed. We're all looking for those stories, relationships, and engagement. The experiences become important. We've been in the mass production phase of history for a long time. We [humans] want to be different from everyone else—there's an expression of ourselves on what we choose to have in our lives, specifically what we put on our bodies. With the customer experience becoming more and more personalized, and with the web everything is customized, it's only natural that eventually this would flow over into product.

Traditional brands can learn a few things from Shoes of Prey:

- Think of ways customers can create their own tailored and personalized products and services.

- Be smarter about your manufacturing and inventory process in order to be more flexible with changing consumer demand.
- Consider catering to your customers who are outliers. Think of what they might need.

Stella & Dot Case Study: Tapping Into the Power of Networks to Sell Products

The Stella & Dot family of brands (Stella & Dot, KEEP Collective, and EVER Skincare) employs a direct-selling model similar to that of Mary Kay, Amway, and Avon. The company works with more than 50,000 women in six countries who sell the Stella & Dot family of brands at their own trunk shows, which they host. These women have earned more than $300 million from running their own flexible businesses, selling more than $1 billion in products. Stella & Dot's mission is to "revolutionize entrepreneurial opportunities for women and men by reinventing the category and creating the modern business opportunity."

I mentioned the show *Undercover Boss* earlier in the book. I recently watched an episode featuring Jessica Herrin, the founder and CEO of Stella & Dot, in which she put on a disguise and pretended she was a reality show contestant as she went behind the scenes of her own company. On the show, you watch Herrin spend time working alongside a customer service agent in the "Delight Center." Stella & Dot, like many companies in the sharing economy, must provide customer service to both sellers of the products and to customers. When I asked Herrin about the reason for the Delight Center, she said,

I think about it as customer experience—our whole mantra is, "Delight is guaranteed." Even if someone wants to return a product . . . we want them to feel so great about it they would still recommend us to a friend afterward. That comes through with our personal styling, the way we train people; we have free and easy try-ons at home with no-pressure styling, and they can shop online. It's all consumer-choice-driven with value add. Across our brands, we've focused on the businesses where that customer experience was broken.

Herrin says that in most retail stores that sell accessories those accessories are hidden behind a glass case where it wasn't easy for customers to try them on or learn how to wear them. She says,

> We improve the experience with the fact you can try it on at home in a no-pressure, no-high-sales kind of way. We'll work hard to make the customer happy in all circumstances. I believe that, to build a sustainable business, you're innovating the experience and making sure that you get not just the sale but the repeat and the referral. We lead with product, product differentiation, product quality, and shopping experience—and, at the end, if there's a problem there better be a real awesome warm human on the phone to love your problem away.

The company's customer base is a highly social group, and Herrin says that Stella & Dot has a dedicated team that is in constant contact with customers via chat and Facebook. She noted in our interview that customers don't want to use the methods companies have hidden in a help section from ten years ago. Customers seek to pick up an app they are already using, and they expect quick service. She added, "We don't want to change customer desires to serve them. We want to scale and efficiently help them where they are and help them love our experience."

As more and more people, especially women, look for flexible work, companies like Stella & Dot will continue to grow and expand into new product categories. These companies can provide opportunities for working mothers that average corporations cannot. Herrin says, "Nine to five just doesn't flatter," and she's right. The idea that your life stops between 9 a.m. and 5 p.m. is not realistic. Companies that create flexible work arrangements for those seeking more flexibility will find that those employees will work even harder because their own ability to make money depends on their work ethic. While it might seem that a person selling products like accessories might run out of people to sell to, that individual will go and train other women, and she will make a profit by growing her own coaching business (setting other women up to sell). The business creates a domino effect, with one positive sale or action setting off a chain of others.

Stella & Dot gives traditional brands a few points to think about:

- Is your employee offering truly compelling or unique?
- How can you provide more unique or flexible hours to your employees?
- How do people learn about your products and services, and how you are engaging your best advocates?

Stella & Dot took a business model that had existed for decades and made it much better by adding a strong digital and marketing component. Today's best companies don't necessarily invent innovative products or services; sometimes, they take an idea that's already out there and make it much better. The company that improves upon a great offering has an advantage because it has no emotional attachment to the original idea, and so it wastes no time innovating.

Amazon, for example, has launched innovations many times over. The company has a leadership principle known as "invent and simplify." As explained to me by one of the first employees on the Amazon leadership team, John Rossman, who was hired to create the third-party seller program,

> Leaders at Amazon expect and require innovation and invention from their teams and always find ways to simplify the processes they touch. They are externally aware, look for new ideas from everywhere, and are not limited by "not invented here" thinking. And they are willing to innovate fearlessly despite the fact that they may be misunderstood for a long time.[3]

Initially, Amazon went head-to-head with eBay, positioning itself as an auction site; however, Amazon found it could not compete with eBay. So,

Amazon quickly pivoted, taking the eBay concept and orienting it toward a successful third-party seller program.[4] Another offering that the company simply improved is Amazon Web Services (AWS). Today, the AWS business is the company's most profitable segment, on its way to becoming a $10 billion-a-year business.[5] Amazon Web Services has thirty different offerings, such as cloud storage, and companies like Pfizer, Intuit, and the U.S. Navy are all using its services. One of Amazon Web Services' first offerings was the Simple Storage Service, which now holds more than 900 billion data objects, with more than a billion new data objects added every day. The platform is self-service—you don't need to talk to a person or negotiate a contract—and you can easily sign up online. AWS is easy to scale up or down. This is a prime example of what Amazon does best. Amazon didn't invent cloud services: it just made the service better.

Amazon's Fulfillment by Amazon (FBA) services, too, provide something unique. In the first decade of Amazon's highly successful reseller business, it had to create physical storage spaces as well as technological systems and processes that optimized product location with the local demand for that product. And Amazon is now better than any other company when it comes to shipping. The company saw a market opportunity to take over the shipping headaches for other companies with a fulfillment service that leveraged the storage and shipping efficiencies it had put in place. Toys "R" Us and Target are among the large companies that hired Amazon to run their e-commerce infrastructures. Amazon picks, packs, and ships products, in addition to providing customer service for the products it handles. In 2013, 73 percent of FBA customers reported that their unit sales on Amazon.com increased by more than 20 percent after joining FBA.[6]

Complacence at Blockbuster

A now-famous quote from a 1999 Blockbuster analyst report reads, "Investor concern over the threat of new technologies is overstated."[7] It must be painful for these analysts to read that today. Blockbuster, started in 1985, had its own period of innovation. At its peak in 2004, the home video rental giant operated 9,000 stores and employed 60,000 people. However, as a result of new entrants into the marketplace, chiefly Netflix and Redbox, the Blockbuster crashed and burned; in 2011, the company and its remaining 1,700 stores were bought at auction for $233 million.[8]

It's clear that complacence ultimately killed Blockbuster, and Netflix—launched in 1998—has no intention of following the same path. But Netflix CEO Reed Hastings did not tread a straightforward path to his founding of the entertainment company. He admits that he got very lucky with his first company, Pure Software, which merged with Atria Software and was later acquired by a larger company; Hastings departed soon after the acquisition. He said, "I had the great fortune of doing a mediocre job at my first company."[9] Hastings attributes his first company's survival to an attitude he learned from whitewater kayaking:

> I was doing whitewater kayaking at the time, and in kayaking if you stare and focus on the problem you are much more likely to hit danger. I focused on the safe water and what I wanted to happen. I didn't listen to the skeptics.[10]

Hastings got the idea for Netflix when he racked up a $40 late fee after forgetting to return *Apollo 13* for six weeks. He found himself wanting to hide this unfortunate news from his wife, and said to himself, "I'm going to compromise the integrity of my marriage over a late fee?" On his way to the gym, he thought about how it had a much better business model—you could exercise for an unlimited amount of time, or not at all, and you were charged one flat fee. Hastings had no idea whether customers would bite for the new business model. Netflix initially started with a single rental service with unlimited rental periods, and thus no late fees, but he wasn't sure customers would even use an online queue.[11]

We know now how the Netflix story unfolded. Today, Netflix continues to innovate, producing powerful series such as *Orange Is the New Black*, *House of Cards*, *Master of None*, *Love*, *Chef's Table*, *Unbreakable Kimmy*

Schmidt, Grace and Frankie, and some amazing comedy specials that have launched the careers of up-and-coming comedians. In 2017 Jerry Seinfeld signed a deal with Netflix that was reportedly worth 100 million dollars for access to "Comedians In Cars Getting Coffee." Netflix has also grown its inventory by getting the rights to compelling shows such as *Jane the Virgin, Arrested Development,* and *Parenthood.* Netflix made it easier than ever to view content, changing the movie industry forever. Why go to the movies when you have the convenience of streaming a film to your flat-screen TV? Why watch a show in prime time on network television when you can see the entire season of a series in one night if you feel like it? The company's practice of releasing a full season of its series simultaneously popularized a new pastime for customers: "binge watching." The company is now in 190 countries and it has more than 75 million subscribers. Its stock has ballooned 500 percent over the past five years. And it all happened because Hastings didn't want to tell his wife about an exorbitant late fee. Now the company is number five on of Fast Company's list of Top 50 Most Innovative Companies of 2016.[12]

***

The best ideas come when people think they can improve something that is inconvenient or not fun. This commonsense disruption (and it's commonsense because, of course, shouldn't we expect X experience to be better?) is happening in every single industry. So if your company is not thinking every day about how you can make life better for your customers, you risk becoming a cautionary tale like Blockbuster. Don't be a company that believes the "threat of new technologies is overstated."

All companies I've discussed in this chapter do more by designing something special, by improving on something already available to customers, or by innovating a completely new product or service. These companies are the disruptors that will benefit and continue to destroy the brands that don't design something special or unique.

Notes

1. John Rossman, *The Amazon Way: 14 Leadership Principles behind the World's Most Disruptive Company* (CreateSpace Independent Publishing Platform, 2014).
2. Alex Fitzpatrick, "Airline: 70,000 Passengers Missed Flights Due to Security Lines," *Time*, May 26, 2016, http://time.com/4349766/airline-70000-passengers-missed-flights-due-to-security-lines/.
3. Rossman, *The Amazon Way*.
4. Ibidem.
5. Dan Frommer, "Amazon Web Services Is Approaching a $10 Billion-a-Year Business," *Recode*, April 28, 2016, www.recode.net/2016/4/28/11586526/aws-cloud-revenue-growth.
6. Rossman, *The Amazon Way*.
7. Vala Afshar, *Twitter Post*, December 20, 2015, 20:00, https://twitter.com/ValaAfshar/status/675752072738955264.
8. *Wikipedia*, s.v. "Blockbuster LLC," last modified November 15, 2016, https://en.wikipedia.org/wiki/Blockbuster_LLC.
9. Michelle Conlin, "Netflix: Recruiting and Retaining the Best Talent," *Bloomberg*, September 14, 2007, www.bloomberg.com/news/articles/2007–09–13/netflix-recruiting-and-retaining-the-best-talentbusinessweek-business-news-stock-market-and-financial-advice.
10. Ray Pride, "Work Out as Little as You Want: Netflix, Ron Howard and White-Water Kayaking," *MSN Blogs*, December 18, 2006, http://moviecitynews.com/2006/12/work-out-as-little-as-you-want-netflix-ron-howard-and-white-water-kayaking/.
11. *Wikipedia*, s.v. "Reed Hastings," last modified November 21, 2016, https://en.wikipedia.org/wiki/Reed_Hastings.
12. "Netlix," *Fast Company*, November 20, 2016, www.fastcompany.com/company/netflix.

CHAPTER 6

Offer a Strong Employee Experience

If the kitchen where the "soup" is made is a miserable work environment, then it's likely the tears of your employees are going to make their way into that soup. Customers are going to be able to taste those tears! The way employees feel at work has an immense impact on the experience of your customers. The reason is twofold. First, really bad things happen to your company when employees don't feel engaged at work. When the people who are building your products and services every day stop caring about the quality of the product, the quality inevitably suffers. It's possible to draw a correlation between low levels of global employee engagement and the state of customer experience. In 2016, Gallup reported that only 32 percent of employees in the United States were engaged—that means they are "involved in, enthusiastic about and committed to their work and workplace." Worldwide, that number drops to a shocking 13 percent.[1]

The second reason happiness levels affect customer experience is more obvious. If a frontline employee hates his job, he's certainly not going to reflect a positive attitude to the customers he is serving. Most of us have been served by a grumpy frontline worker, whether it's a salesperson, an agent (on the phone or in person), or even a health care employee like a nurse or doctor. If an individual isn't happy at work, he's probably not going to smile at the customer, go the extra mile for the customer, and or be empathetic toward the customer. We're all human. We all understand what it feels like to have a bad day, but when all the company's employees appear to be having bad days all the time, one has to wonder what's going on in that company. On the other hand, happy employees have more energy for customers. They smile easily, are sociable, and are more prone to be empathetic to the customer.

Part of creating a great place to work is treating your employees like they're smart. In fact, your employees are an incredible source of knowledge when it comes to improving your products, processes, and services. According to the authors of *Service Design for Business: A Practical Guide to Optimizing the Customer Experience*,

> Employees have extremely detailed knowledge about what creates value for customers and what works for the business. Involving customer-facing staff in creative design helps decrease your chances of failure. The significant by-product is highly engaged staff that will embrace the improvement and change they were part of creating.

Other good practices include avoiding the use of scripts and giving employees resources that will allow them to satisfy the customer—in the contact center world, we call this service recovery. Not only is this practice good for the customer experience, but it makes the frontline worker feel great too. Who wants to say no to customers all day? This practice is not only about empowering the employee to make the customer's day by giving her the authority to move the needle for the customer: it's about giving employees access to the technology they need to do their jobs well. Customers seek to use the technology they prefer in their personal lives when contacting a company, and employees also prefer to use at work the technologies they use at home. Finally, a good CRM system should make life amazing for both customers and employees. The entire point of upgrading business technology is to make work better for the employees. But instead of replacing that old CRM from the 1980s, companies continue to pile on more and more technology. Employees are forced to sign in and out of many different systems in a given day. This is stressful for the employee and it slows interactions with customers to the speed of molasses! To create an outstanding customer experience, the company must provide modern technology that enables employees to do their jobs without much fuss.

Employee Experiences Are Critical

Brands that create knock-your-socks-off employee experiences boast higher stock prices and overall growth. According to an article in *USA Today*, "there's fairly solid evidence that companies that treat employees well see their stocks prosper."[2] Examples include Google, a company that's seen its stock price balloon more than 674 percent since 2004. Google is famous for its employee practices, which include ensuring that employees are never more than 200 feet from food, and the food is free. Employees have access to bowling alleys, swimming pools, and college reimbursement plans. If an employee dies, Google will pay 50 percent of the deceased employee's salary for a decade.

Julie Gebauer, managing director for talent and rewards at Towers Watson, a global professional services company, says, "The data strongly supports the fact that organizations that focus on the engagement of their employees deliver stronger performance. It's not just making them happy—that's not a business issue. Engagement is."[3] Yet a 2015 Gallup study found that only 32 percent of U.S. workers were engaged.[4] That means almost 70 percent of workers are disengaged. That's most people! Can you imagine how that's hurting your company?

Clearly, most employees don't feel valued at work. In a Deloitte study, 87 percent of organizations cited culture and engagement as one of their top challenges.[5] Perhaps leadership should start by inviting their employees to have candid conversations with them. The employees should be able to provide anonymous feedback so they speak the truth without fear of being fired. It's critical, though, that leaders have a pulse on what's going on with their employees—whether the news is pleasant or unpleasant. The point is that it absolutely matters that your employees feel happy and valued at work. Doesn't it make sense that if employees feel their work is valued, their work will be better? The products and services will be better. The employees will whistle while they work. They will have smiles on their faces. According to the *USA Today* article, publicly traded companies on the Fortune 100 Best Companies to Work For list have gained an average 10.8 percent a year since 1998.[6]

There is no place that employee dissatisfaction poses a greater threat than in the contact centers, the places where customers are most likely to make direct contact with the brand. The contact center—seen as a cost center—is the place where your agents are recipients of what can be a lot of negativity. Their job is to fix problems. Generally, the company itself does not value the contact center staff because the contact center is not viewed as a revenue generator. The staff can tell that they aren't valued, and guess who is going to hear that in their voice or their digital communications? Your customers! Have you ever been on a customer service call when you heard an abrasive tone, or perhaps a passive-aggressive tone? I can assure you these employees don't like their jobs, and they certainly don't feel valued at work.

Most companies have strict processes and procedures for their contact centers, and customer service agents are given scripts to follow. If a customer needs something outside the standard offering, she is out of luck. Agents are not allowed to help customers with unique requests or issues, even if they want to. But companies that refuse to consider that customers' needs must be addressed in a variety of ways are shooting themselves in the foot. In your personal life, you know that life happens—not every problem unfolds in accordance with a script. But at work, many employees are not empowered to do anything to address idiosyncratic problems if it could cost the company more money. This isn't true of all companies, but it is true of most.

Only a handful of companies account for "life happening." The customer-facing employees at these remarkable companies are trained to listen to what customers truly need, and these employees have budgets and freedom to help the customer with requests that are not part of the standard script. These are the companies that have "surprise and delight" budgets—they understand and invest in individual customers and customer stories. But this approach is for the brave few, those CEOs who aren't stressed out by quarterly profits. I know you had to read that sentence twice—it sounds weird, doesn't it? Because quarterly profits are very important! They are, except when you are thinking about the long game. Companies that take a long view understand that profound customer experiences are critical to brand building. CEOs who get this invest in programs that will cement customer loyalty over the long term. It's much easier for me to say that, however, than it is for a CEO to explain to investors why making less in the short term could bring greater profits in the long term.

So why do some companies have amazing cultures, while others do not? Why are companies like Zappos, Nordstrom, and Ritz-Carlton getting all the press and recognition when it comes to incredible employee and customer experiences (and the subsequent business benefits)? The good news is that these companies started with exactly what you have. In fact, we all have access to the same set of tools and capabilities, and we are all capable of the same results, but the mentality of company leaders makes all the difference. The leaders' mindset creates the company culture—and it's hard to stray from that culture once it exists. A turnaround can happen, but it takes discipline and support at the most influential levels of the company.

Working at Airbnb

Here's the thing about customer experience: you cannot talk about it without looking inside the place where it's built. Often, the customer experience will tell us everything we need to know about what it's actually like to work at the company. Frustrating or amazing, the customer experience is a reflection of the employee experience. Let's talk about what it's like to work at Airbnb. First, if you visit Airbnb, you'll see that its offices are among the most thoughtfully designed and creative spaces in corporate America. Every room at the headquarters is inspired by an actual Airbnb listing somewhere in the world.

Once home to a San Francisco jewelry mart, the Airbnb office is set up so that employees can work wherever they want. The 72,000 square feet of funky and aesthetically pleasing space has been transformed to reflect an employee's dream work station. And it's no accident that the employee digs are as amazing as they are: the founders of Airbnb value design thinking.

Design is a big part of every physical and conceptual aspect of Airbnb, from the design of employee experiences to the design of customer experiences.

In fact, two of the three Airbnb founders—Joe Gebbia and Brian Chesky—met while they were attending the Rhode Island School of Design (RISD).[7] Acknowledging that employees work at a desk for most of the day, Gebbia says, "We spend the majority of our lives at work. Why wouldn't it be as comfortable or as inspiring as your own home?" One example of this atmosphere is the focus on round tables: "It's less hierarchical and more collaborative," Gebbia says. The design reflects the company's culture and values, and helps new ideas get their time in the sun, no matter who puts them forth.

While Airbnb bakes experience into the design of everything it does, many companies today put employees in depressing offices with little inspiration, little sunlight, and little thought about how those employees are going to feel in their cubicles every day. If you want your customer to have an incredible customer experience, make sure that the people who build those experiences feel comfortable and happy at work. You cannot talk about customer experience without looking at what's going on deep within the company to create that experience.

Traditional brands can learn from companies like Airbnb that

- The brand is just as accountable for the experience it provides to employees as it is for the one it provides to its customers.
- Being obsessed with the customer journey early on can save your company from problems down the road.
- Creating new markets prevents your products from being commoditized.

It may not be all rainbows and butterflies at companies that take design seriously, but they've got the infrastructure to fix what they don't like about the customer experience. Take, for example, Uber. For all Uber's success, the company has also had a lot of challenges, with regard to both its reputation and its customer experience. The company is embroiled in legal battles over its autonomy in its practice of hiring drivers. Both Uber and competitor Lyft recently left

Austin, Texas, over a fight with the government—Uber wanted to continue to handle its own background checks on drivers, and the city wanted control over the process. Austin citizens were left angry and drivers were left without jobs.[8]

These ride-sharing services are not without their own internal challenges. Drivers are sometimes accused of cancelling rides, or worse. Additionally, there is an ongoing fight between Uber and drivers over their employment status. It's not rare for Uber to face class action lawsuits from drivers who want the benefits that employees get. At the heart of the matter is essentially the pay. By the time Uber drivers take care of vehicle maintenance, gasoline, insurance, and the cut Uber takes, many feel they aren't compensated enough. However, even with all these challenges, Uber continues to expand. Companies in the sharing economy are experiencing growing pains as they aggressively scale and expand despite roadblocks and unflattering press along the way. This is the customer experience challenge for such companies: Do they sacrifice quality as demand grows all over the world for their services?[9]

Brands that have been around for twenty years or more are simply not innovating at the rate of these newer brands. Companies that operate in the on-demand or sharing economies are not purely taking a product or service and making it better: they are changing the game entirely.

Whether you are a CEO or an intern, you, personally, know and understand what a good customer experience is. You've had them. On the other hand, you can probably also recount a recent customer experience that left a bad taste in your mouth. But when we show up for work each day, something prevents us from making decisions as if we were on the receiving end of a customer experience. In fact, most executives would benefit from knowing exactly what it's like to work at their company and with their company—no sugarcoating!

***

There's no way to avoid investing in your workplace if you want to create a compelling customer experience. Step one is looking at your employees' experience—what it is actually like to work at your company at all levels. You have heard that in an emergency situation on an airplane, the adult should put a mask on himself before assisting a child, right? It's the same principle for building customer experiences. You simply cannot create a good experience for a customer unless the people who are building that experience have what they need to do their jobs. In the next chapter, we will look at how great companies leverage innovation in technology on both the employee and customer sides of the equation, and how these technologies make them more successful.

Notes

1. Annamarie Mann and Jim Harter, "The Worldwide Employee Engagement Crisis," *Gallup Business Journal*, January 7, 2016, www.gallup.com/businessjournal/188033/worldwide-employee-engagement-crisis.aspx.
2. John Waggoner, "Do Happy Workers Mean Higher Company Profits?" *USA Today*, February 20, 2013, www.usatoday.com/story/money/personalfinance/2013/02/19/treating-employees-well-stock-price/1839887/.
3. Ibidem.
4. "Employee Engagement in U.S. Stagnant in 2015," *Gallup*, January 13, 2016, www.gallup.com/poll/188144/employee-engagement-stagnant-2015.aspx.
5. David Brown, Veronica Melian, Marc Solow, Sonny Chheng, and Kathy Parker, "Culture and Engagement: The Naked Organization," *Deloitte University Press*, February 27, 2015, https://dupress.deloitte.com/dup-us-en/focus/human-capital-trends/2015/employee-engagement-culture-human-capital-trends-2015.html.
6. John Waggoner, "Do Happy Workers Mean Higher Profits?" *USA Today*, February 20, 2013, www.usatoday.com/story/money/personalfinance/2013/02/19/treating-employees-well-stock-price/1839887/.
7. Eva Hagberg, "Rooms with a View," *Metropolis*, December 2013, www.metropolismag.com/December-2013/Rooms-with-a-View/index.php?cparticle=3&siarticle=2#artanc.
8. Eliana Dockterman, "Uber and Lyft Are Leaving Austin after Losing Background Check Vote," *TIME*, May 8, 2016, http://fortune.com/2016/05/08/uber-lyft-leaving-austin/.
9. Ben Handleman, "Class Action Lawsuit: Wisconsin Uber Drivers Sue Uber," *FOX 6 Now*, June 24, 2016, http://fox6now.com/2016/06/24/class-action-lawsuit-wisconsin-uber-drivers-sue-uber.

CHAPTER 7

Modernize With Technology

Alan Trefler, CEO and founder of Pegasystems, articulated to me one day over coffee the problem with today's technology landscape and the way buyers interact with it. He sums it up as a software problem. He calls this the "run out of runway problem." Buyers can be seduced by beautiful demos and artfully created marketing content, but, according to Trefler, many of these solutions are illusions. He suggests that companies look at the architecture from a business perspective and ask a few important questions:

1. Will this technology let me accommodate the differences in my business if we sell a variety of products and services to different types of customers, such as B2C and B2B?
2. What if my business becomes more complicated over time?
3. What if my customer base segments in ways I don't anticipate?
4. What if I have to merge and a new organization has to be brought on?
5. Does the platform have the flexibility to run the way I need it to run, where I need it to run, and with the breadth I need?

These are high-level questions that need to be addressed with the company's leadership—and they underline that basing technology buying decisions in, for example, the contact center alone, without collaborating among leadership and business units, is dangerous. A strong technology program needs to be continually iterated over time as business needs change.

A multitude of technologies are changing the opportunity brands have to provide better customer experiences. These technologies support CRM, personalization, analytics/data, and other capabilities that allow the company to be increasingly relevant to the customer—to offer the right experience and the right content at the right time.

Technology's Effect on the Employee Experience

Aaron Levie, CEO of Box, once tweeted, "Enterprise software used to be about making existing work more efficient. Now the opportunity for software is to transform the work itself." Knowing how complicated the digital landscape is today, it's no surprise that most big brands have complex technology stacks. Employees' technology lives are much more complicated at work than they are at home. Because of the slow rate of technology adoption as well as security concerns, many employees are not allowed to use their personal devices in the workplace. So, while this book looks at customer experience, as I discussed in the last chapter, we absolutely cannot do so without examining the employee experience as well.

The Curse of Old CRM Technology

Customer experience leaders are challenged not only by the complicated landscape, but by the limits that the internal technology places on a seamless operation. For example, many brands have old CRM technology, much of which was implemented in the early 1980s. A customer relationship management tool should help the company analyze a customer's history to provide better service and, in so doing, improve customer satisfaction and loyalty. CRM systems should compile data from all your different channels, including newer ones such as social and mobile.

Brands wish vendors took more time to understand the lay of the land. Many brands are frustrated that vendors don't know how certain tools would integrate with other technologies. Another challenge is the fact that many out-of-the-box solutions will cover only 60 percent of the client's needs—the other 40 percent must be customized at an additional cost. Practitioners—customer experience leaders at top global brands—seek tools that are easy to set up, and that don't require much hand-holding from the vendor after the initial implementation.

Not only do practitioners seek technologies that are turnkey, but they also seek tools that don't require a lot of tedious work from employees. In the contact center, employees frequently must manually tag and delegate escalation incidents, when customers want to be referred to someone at a higher level. Dan Moriarty, former director of social strategy and activation for Hyatt, and current director of digital for the Chicago Bulls, told me about his technology challenge while at Hyatt.[1] He said,

> There is a huge opportunity to extend more help to brands like Hyatt, ones focused on emotional connections, with efficiencies and integrations so our people have more time to focus on personalization and less on transactions. We want to reduce the workload on our 24–7 social care team on things such as tagging content, making requests across systems, and identifying guests in CRMs, so they can simply be human and engage in real conversations with customers on their terms.

Moriarty wants the agent to have more time to spend on engagement with the customer, rather than tagging and inputting customer information and content on many different forms. Often, when it comes to different channels, employees are charged with copying and pasting content from one channel into a CRM for another channel. This task is highly time consuming for agents, and they should not have to do it. Agents spend too much time completing tasks that are better suited to machines.

Good CRM Is Everything to Agent Experiences

On the bright side, good technology can make agents' lives much better. For example, a good CRM will not bring up a customer's history right away, but it will tell the agent recent moves the customer made on both in-store and digital channels. The best customer experiences are highly personalized, but most technology offerings do not allow that type of personalization to scale easily for brands. Consider Barb Rechterman, chief customer officer of GoDaddy, who, when I asked about challenges of the customer experience vendor landscape, told me,

> The key to building a good company is to understand your customers—who they are, specifically, what they need, who their customers are. Technology is great, we love it, but what technology companies need is that personal touch, the human connection. At GoDaddy, our product core is technology, but one of the things that keeps our customers coming back, and recommending us to their friends and family, is the personalized telephone support.

When you are creating highly personalized experiences, a good CRM system makes all the difference. An ideal CRM database works on behalf of the agent to pull in useful information about the customer. For example, the CRM can tell the agent local information such as the weather where the customer lives, any personal facts the company has about the customer, and, if IoT is embedded, information such as whether the customer is driving or doing another task while contacting the company. That way, the agent can better tailor the experience for that customer.

Technology Needs of the Blended Team

Today, we're seeing more and more blended teams—meaning, the teams are serving customers on a variety of channels. You don't have one team managing social media and another team managing phone calls. Employees are handling a variety of channels for that customer. Customer experience leaders would like vendors to create technology that offers a unified work-flow. Such technology would allow the agent to pop in and offer service to the customer, regardless of the channel. The agent could cross-reference data from a variety of channels, so the customer does not have to repeat information. Most customers have become used to the drudgery of contacting customer service and repeating themselves every time. Employees who serve customers are stuck with antiquated technologies and have become used to the verbal abuse from customers who are tired of being provided with terrible experiences. If the CEO and his reports were the ones who had to serve customers directly, day in and day out, one has to wonder whether outdated technologies would be tolerated in the contact center and other areas of the business.

***

Technology is incredibly important in our lives, at home and at work. It has improved our lives in virtually every way possible, but too often companies aren't thoughtful about the technology they bring into the workplace, and that affects the employee experience and, in turn, the customer experience. The technology strategy has to, first, consider the experience of the employee and, second, the customer. Today's companies leverage self-service technology, but what happens when the self-service technology isn't up to par?

Note

1. Blake Morgan, *A Practitioner's View: 20 Top Brands Address Their Challenges with the Customer Experience Vendor Landscape* (Oakland: Self-published, 2016).

CHAPTER 8

Obsess Over the Customer

As a teenager in Orange County, California, if you're not playing sports, in school, or doing homework, you're probably at the mall. I loved going to Nordstrom, where the beautiful fashions transported me to a world of savvy (literally, the name of one of the women's departments). No longer was I an awkward teenage girl with braces. I was a modern woman bedecked in the most stunning new trends. A big part of shopping was fantasy. Let's be real: I couldn't afford many of these clothes on my allowance, but I loved going to the department store and the way it made me feel.

On special occasions, like graduation and prom, I was allowed to buy something from Nordstrom. One day, in preparation for prom, I went with my mom to Nordstrom and purchased the most beautiful pair of platform shoes. They were very trendy, and I had been drooling over them for months—they were a perfect match to the dress I had bought for the occasion. I was ready for prom. I had the date and the outfit, and I was even splurging to get my makeup and hair done. Things took a turn for the worse, however, when I came home one day to find the Nordstrom shoe box torn open and a few bites in the heel of the shoe. The perpetrator? Our mischievous dog, Dottie, a rescued Dalmatian that took her anxiety out on our furniture. I was defeated. These were expensive shoes, and now they were ruined! So, we climbed into my mom's car and drove back to Nordstrom to see what could be done. We had absolutely zero expectations—we only knew I had no shoes for prom.

What happened next was fairly unheard of. The salesperson took one look at the shoes after we explained what happened and, with a big smile, said, "Sure, we'll just replace them for you." My jaw dropped. "You're going to take back this pair of shoes that are now ruined and it was our fault?" I said. But that's exactly what happened. Nordstrom ate the cost of those shoes, but the store gained a customer for life.

Other companies have mirrored this no-questions-asked return policy. Zappos is one company that has a similar policy. Are these liberal return policies costing the companies that offer them a ton of money? Aren't customers using the products and returning them right afterward, taking advantage of the company's generosity? It turns out, when you examine the cost of service recovery, nickel-and-diming your customers and having a no-questions-asked returns policy ends up costing the same amount.[1] That doesn't take into account all the good word of mouth you will generate—whether through a Yelp! review, a story told to friends and family, or even a tweet—when you provide your customers with a good experience.

Designing Obsessively Thoughtful User Experiences

Customers know how much or how little you value them by their interactions with your brand. These interactions are marked in customers' minds by how easy it is for them to buy from you, to how easy it is to use the product, and how much they can interact with you and your products via their preferred channels and devices.

User experience is an increasingly key piece of customer experience because more of our experiences are digital. We are building experiences via technology that move a customer through a funnel, and we may never even make in-person contact with them. The word *user* is terrible because it takes away the human element of a customer. However, user is the name we've given human beings who do business with us. This is especially true from a technology perspective.

It's easy to confuse customer experience with user experience, but they are very different. User experience is a piece of customer experience, and it's important to differentiate the two. *Customer experience is the relationship you build with customers through the series of interactions you have with them.*

Customer experience is measured differently than user experience: metrics include overall experience, likelihood of customers to continue use, and likelihood that they will recommend the product or service to others.

User experience, on the other hand, has to do with the way people interact with your product and *the experience they receive from that interaction.* User experience metrics have more to do with the way the customer uses your digital offering. These metrics include success rate, error rate, abandonment rate, time to a complete task, and clicks to completion. User experiences have to do with, for example, the customer's ability to seek information on the website briskly and without frustration. In contrast, a good customer experience makes the customer happy with the overall interaction he's had with the company. The customer should feel he had a pleasant, professional, helpful interaction and should feel pleased with the overall exchange. Your business can have the most amazing advertising, marketing, and sales efforts, but if the company falls short on the customer's interaction with the website or mobile app, or if software issues or other problems hinder the customer from completing any associated task, the overall customer experience fails.

A good user experience in 2017 is imperative. When we talk about customer experience, we don't highlight user experience enough. *Customer experience is not about the extra bells and whistles of the offering, but it's about the offering itself.* Customers seek experiences that make their lives easier. They are not looking to be wined and dined with extras: they're looking for companies that make life easier for them.

The Evolution of Customer Service

Everyone works hard in the beginning of a relationship—after all, you want to attract your desired mate. But how hard do you work after the other person has expressed interest and started seeing you? Most companies treat customers like they are yesterday's news—once they have the sale (or they've seduced the buyer), the effort decreases. Proof is in the resources and staffing the company devote to customer care—no company would understaff its sales department or its marketing team, but it's normal to understaff the contact center. If this wasn't the case, you would never wait on hold for long stretches of time to reach a person. However, long hold times are the norm for current customers who were sold a product and need help with it. Consider this infograph I've created, "The Evolution of Customer Service":

The Evolution of Customer Service

THE PAST			THE FUTURE
Technology Makes Experience Worse			Technology Makes Experience Better
Open 9-5 x 5			Open 24x7
Company is in control of where interaction happens			Customer is in control of where interaction happens
Customer Repeats Information On Every Channel			Company Knows Information From Every Channel
Call Center Volume Is High			Mobile Messaging Volume Is High
Customer Finds Content			Content Finds Customer
Customer Fixes Product			Product Fixes Product
Agent Works In Ten Systems			Agent Works Through One System
Customer Service Has No Budget			Customer Service Gets Marketing's Budget

BLAKEMORGAN
www.blakemichellemorgan.com

Figure 8.1 *The Evolution of Customer Service*

Technology Makes Experience Worse Versus Technology Makes Experience Better

In the past, technology seemed to make customer experiences worse rather than better—and this happens even today. It's not rare that you call a company for help and are met by hard-of-hearing interactive voice response

(IVR) technology. The technology is meant to save companies money, and perhaps it does in the short term, but it creates highly frustrating experiences for customers. Often, customers will enter extensive information via the IVR, only to be asked the same information when they finally reach a person. Some companies make the mistake of not allowing customers to opt out of the IVR (usually accomplished by pressing zero). Customers feel like companies will do whatever they can to avoid engaging with customers. In the future, companies will use technology to assist customers, but the technology's ability to listen and interpret what the customer needs will improve. Technology isn't necessarily a bad thing when it comes to service, but it has to work well. Today's technology often doesn't.

Open 9–5 Versus Open 24–7

Even in your own time zone, problems don't stop at five o'clock in the evening. In fact, many people work from nine in the morning until five without an opportunity to take care of the problems that arise in their lives. Also, consider the fact that we now operate in a global economy—what message does it send people in other locales when a company operates only during hours that are friendly to the company's own time zone? Today's companies cannot afford to be open only for customers who happen to live in their local time zone. They need to be available for customers twenty-four hours a day, seven days a week. Social media and instant messaging have only added to the pressure to be open nights and weekends. We live and work in an always-on world, and you need to prepare for that.

Who Controls Where the Interaction Happens?

In the past, companies were able to avoid working very hard to help customers. Companies interacted with customers via the call center or even snail mail. Then e-mail grew in popularity as a method of communication, then chat, then social media. But companies approach social media and nontraditional channels in the same way they approached the call center in the 1980s; back then, they staffed the call center, put up a "sign," and waited for customers to find them.

Look, for example, at the way most brands are serving customers on Twitter:

@Nikesupport
@FitbitSupport
@ComcastCares
@AppleSupport
@ChaseSupport
@XboxSupport
@VZWSupport
@AskTarget
@UPSHelp
@AmazonHelp
@NeftlixHelps
@BestBuySupport
@SpotifyCares

Figure 8.2 *Customer Service Channels*

Rather than simply serving customers where the customers are, brands are still setting up "centers," and customers have to know how to tag those brands to get help. What if I don't know how to tag the brand in my tweet?

As the number of social and messaging channels increases, brands will need to work harder to find the customers who need help rather than the other way around. Brands simply cannot control the channels or the way they interact with customers who need help. They will need to ensure that they have a very strong outreach program through keywords and powerful searches across every channel. The days of brand control are over.

Must the Customer Repeat Information?

Omnichannel is an approach that aims to engage the customer on a variety of channels and provide a seamless experience across the platforms. The idea is that the customer would be able to move effortlessly among the retail store, the website properties, and the mobile applications, and have one experience no matter where she is. Omni literally means "all," and the omnichannel approach encompasses the idea that you have one experience across many properties. While many companies pursue this goal today, in reality, it's a fairy tale the business world dreams about. No company has fully proven its ability to know every move the customer makes in real time. A recent study surveyed 7,000 consumers and found that, in the last six months, 60 percent of online shoppers made purchases that involved them shopping and learning about the product on multiple channels; however, 87 percent said that brands must work harder to create a seamless experience for customers.[2]

In an ideal scenario, the customer can send a message on any channel, and the brand can track the customer's moves in real time. In the real world, though, when customers contact a company, they need to provide a litany of details about who they are, along with specific information about what they're calling about. Ideally, the company already has a ton of data on the customer before the customer calls in. The agent, through data delivered via a connected device, knows what the customer is doing without the customer having to explain himself. In the future, companies will have better tools and be able to see what the customer needs help with as they need it, with much less repeating of information on the customer's end.

When the Volume Is High

As the generations that prefer to use digital methods of contacting brands come of age, brands will continue to see volumes change. A 2014 Gallup poll confirmed that text messages now outrank phone calls as the dominant form of communication among millennials. That's just millennials. For generation Z, the numbers are even more extreme. Texting among eighteen- to twenty-four-year-olds soared from 600 to more than 1,400 texts a month.[3]

Millennials and generation Z do not want to have to call you. Messaging apps like Snapchat, WhatsApp, and Kik are increasingly popular, as is traditional texting. Brands need to prepare for this move toward messaging by investing in technology that will allow them to create a presence on messaging apps.

Customer Finds Content Versus Content Finds Customer

It's not rare for companies to post too much information on their website for customers to wade through. In fact, not only do many customers Google questions for their products and services, but customer service agents are doing the same. Why use a company's internal knowledge base when it's easier to Google? A recent survey on web self-service conducted by Forrester found that self-service is now the most widely used communication channel for customer service, surpassing voice for the first time.[4] This means that customers would rather fix problems themselves than contact your brand. So, how can brands create more personalized content for customers? All too often, companies create mass content that doesn't cater to a customer's specific needs. For example, it's not rare for a customer to send a tweet to a brand, and for that brand to send the customer a link to a community thread on the topic. The customer then has to search through that community thread for an answer. It's a lot of work. Customers don't want to have to read through hundreds of pages of text to find the one piece of information they're looking for.

The good news is that in the future products will be smarter. The products themselves will be able to predict what customers need and send them just-in-time content to address that need. The Internet of Things will help make such service a reality. We still have a way to go before content starts finding customers, but with the rapid advances in technology, it could soon become a reality.

Streamlining Systems

When you call customer service and it seems to take forever for the agent to help you, it's likely that she is switching through different pieces of technology to get to the right information. Forget about the customer experience for a minute, can you imagine how stressful this process is for the employee? Companies often have a few different vendors to address their various technology needs, and as a result, employees are signing in and out of a number of different tools. Today's customer service team needs to follow the customer through various channels. Contact centers are starting to move toward blended teams, where one agent on the team is working on a few different channels on a given day. Agents benefit from a "unified workflow," which unites all the different environments the agent needs to navigate. It's better for the employee experience, so it is, in turn, better for the customer experience.

***

Most of what I talk about in this chapter involves resources. In the past, the contact center was seen purely as a cost center rather than as a direct revenue source. However, more executives are making the connection between customer loyalty and customer service that nurtures customer relationships.

Customer service is even getting new names at some companies, especially those in the tech industry. Examples include the "Customer Happiness Team," "Customer Success Team," or "Customer Delight Team." If customers have great experiences, they talk about those experiences, referring friends and family to the company that impressed them. Additionally they are influencing mass amounts of total strangers through online reviews. Customer service is tasked with handling more and more of the cross-channel engagement that is occurring, whether that is handling a customer service question or a listening to a customer's response to a marketing campaign. Customer service will continue to evolve as a critical component of a competitive business strategy, and in the future, this group will have more resources and influence to be able to champion the customer for the business.

Notes

1. Mark Weinstein (SVP and Global Head of Customer Engagement, Loyalty and Partnerships for Hilton Worldwide), in discussion with the author.
2. Nick Peart, "2014: The Year of Omnichannel Customer Service," *ZenDesk*, November 25, 2013, www.zendesk.com/blog/omnichannel-2014.
3. Neil Howe, "Why Millennials Are Texting More and Talking Less," *Forbes*, July 15, 2015, www.forbes.com/sites/neilhowe/2015/07/15/why-millennials-are-texting-more-and-talking-less/#4cc637965576.
4. Kate Leggett, "Forrester's Top Trends for Customer Service in 2015," *Forrester*, December 17, 2014, http://blogs.forrester.com/kate_leggett/14-12-17-forresters_top_trends_for_customer_service_in_2015.

CHAPTER 9

Reward Responsibility and Accountability

It used to be impossible to do business without seeing a customer's face. But today, businesses are increasingly separated from the customers they're serving. It's easy to be company centric and ignore the individual not present in the room—the customer—when decisions are being made. I speak extensively about Amazon because it is a company that engineered a positive customer experience from the first seed planted in the early 2000s. Jeff Bezos started putting an empty chair in meetings for the customer at a time when this wasn't a widely practiced activity.

Here's another great Amazon best practice: all managers must train in the call center every year. If you're lucky, you might call Amazon customer service on the right day and get Jeff Bezos on the phone. Amazon audit its customer experiences. Jeff Bezos, in his letter to shareholders in April 2013, said:

> We build automated systems that look for occasions when we've provided a customer experience that isn't up to our standards . . . one industry observer recently received an automated email from us that said, "We noticed that you experienced poor video playback while watching . . . Casablanca. We're sorry for the inconvenience and have issued you a refund.

This letter from Bezos shows true responsibility and accountability. Amazon puts its customer's experience ahead of profits. While many companies are aware that a successful service recovery can spawn twenty times the positive word of mouth that regular advertising delivers, they'd rather turn a blind eye to poor experiences. If the customer doesn't complain, it's not their responsibility, right?

A CEO's worst nightmare should be the 95 percent of unhappy customers who don't complain.[1] Customers who don't complain to your contact center might save you a few dollars today, but eventually those customers will disappear without a trace and they'll tell their friends and family not to do business with you. You will never know what happened until you see your sales numbers plummeting. And this is why the most customer-centric companies continue to profit. Research by Deloitte and Touche found that customer-centric companies are 60 percent more profitable than those not focused on the customer.[2]

Another Amazon example involves four thousand pink iPods the company ordered to stock for Christmas. About one month before Christmas, Apple contacted Amazon and indicated that it would not make the Christmas delivery. Apple made a technical change to the iPod and decided to only ship new iPods with the updated technology; Apple noted that once it received the new technology to make the iPods, it would send the pink iPods, but that wouldn't happen by Christmas.

How many companies have you done business with that have not delivered on a promise and blamed the supplier? I can name a handful of companies that, in just the last two years, blamed outside factors on their inability to deliver on time. Instead of adopting an attitude of blame, Amazon bought 4,000 pink iPods at retail price. It repacked them and shipped them to Amazon customers who had ordered pink iPods and were expecting them in time for Christmas. The company lost a lot of money on that sale, but Amazon was okay eating the cost—maintaining the commitment to customers was what was important. Apple later agreed to split the cost difference with Amazon, but Amazon didn't know that when its executives made the decision to eat the cost in order to fulfill customers' expectations. This is precisely why Amazon has the customer loyalty it enjoys today. Customers trust that Amazon will always deliver on its promise, no excuses.

Governance Helps With Accountability

While it's crucial for a company to be responsible and accountable to its customers, it must also be accountable to its stakeholders. These include employees, vendor partners, the community in which the company does business, and, *last*, investors. Too many brands, large and small, put investors first—and this practice gets in the way of their success. Investors are often looking for short-term gains, and this focus becomes a hindrance to innovation, a subject I will talk more about in the next chapter.

When you are responsible and accountable to the broader group of stakeholders, not just your board, you operate a business based on a set of values, and these values will not be swayed by short-term thinking. In *Outside In: The Power of Putting Customers at the Center of Your Business*, Kerry Bodine and Harley Manning discuss the role governance plays within organizations to create a culture of accountability. Governance within your company will create a series of checks and balances by assigning responsibilities. It essentially involves delegating customer experience management tasks to certain roles within the company and ensuring that groups are collaborating across the company to achieve those tasks.

Bodine and Manning encourage companies to create a consistent set of customer experience standards This includes setting criteria to evaluate project funding and prioritizing business decisions. Governance can help to maintain a stable queue of customer experience improvement projects and assess the progress of those programs regularly. These customer experience programs must receive close attention—they may need to be reconstructed when there are new policies, products, technologies, business processes, or external factors that affect the customer experience.

The governance structure will ensure that there are groups and individuals responsible for a piece of the customer experience, and that everyone knows how and where they contribute. This way, when something goes wrong, it's not hard to find the root of the issue. It also decreases the unfavorable customer experiences that will hurt your brand. Executive involvement in the programs can include steering committees and coaching of customer-facing teams. All of these pursuits contribute positively to your customer experience governance structure. In *Outside In*, the authors also cite an example from Canada Post, an organization that requires all budget requests to address ten customer-focused questions before money is allocated. The main question is: "How is this going to benefit the customer?" Responsibility and accountability are not just about organizing your business in a way that makes you a customer-focused company, but they are about standing up for your values. If you want to be competitive in tomorrow's marketplace, you need to understand that being a good global citizen is important.

Being a Good Global Citizen

The year 2016 was a rough one in global news. A tumultuous American election, Brexit, ISIS, Syria, climate change, poverty, murder, racism, lack of female representation at the highest levels of business, a rancorous political season—there's enough to make you pretty bummed out about the state of the world.

The thing is, businesses have greater power and more resources than the average person. It's business's responsibility to make decisions that are good for all organisms living on this planet. Not all people have the luxury of caring about the world around them—they are too busy just surviving. Those in leadership positions at companies must make decisions that are in the best interest of the company and its customers, but they are also responsible for making decisions that preserve the environment and sustain future generations. The better, faster, cheaper ride that many businesses are still on is going to destroy the planet. It's not sustainable. We need companies to take leadership positions by putting their money where their mouth is. We don't need more polluting products or practices. We need to be careful about where our products are made, that the people making them are treated fairly, and that the places where we do business are humane places. It is possible to be successful and not destructive. Many of you reading this have kids, and some of you may even have grandkids. What kind of world do you want to leave to them? It matters.

Corporate Social Activism

Whether you are republican or democrat, you need to understand the business decisions you make have an impact on the communities around you. Today CEOs are in the spotlight than at any point in history, thanks to social media. Every action that a CEO makes can affect their customer-base and make a statement to society about what the company will and won't stand for.

One such company is Salesforce, among the largest vendors of CRM products. Marc Benioff, CEO and cofounder of Salesforce, makes a habit of taking stances against what he sees as policies that threaten the freedoms of Americans, many of whom are his customers. Benioff, once a Republican but now not affiliated with any political party, has advocated for the rights of gay and transgender people, saying anti-gay positions are anti-business. Indiana recently passed a law called the Religious Freedom Restoration Act that enabled businesses to discriminate against customers because of their sexual orientation or gender identity. The week it was passed, one pizza restaurant refused to cater the wedding of a gay couple.[3] In response to this new law, nine CEOs, from Angie's List, Salesforce Marketing Cloud, Anthem Inc., Eli Lilly and Company, Cummins, Emmis Communications, Roche Diagnostics, Indiana University Health, and Dow AgroSciences, called on the Republican leadership to enact legislation to prevent "discrimination based upon sexual orientation or gender identity."[4]

Other CEOs also announced their disappointment with the law, among them Tim Cook of Apple Inc., PayPal cofounder Max Levchin, and Yelp CEO Jeremy Stoppelman. Stoppelman said, "[It] is unconscionable to imagine that Yelp would create, maintain, or expand a significant business presence in any state that encouraged discrimination by businesses against our employees, or consumers at large." The NCAA (the National Collegiate

Athletic Association) which was holding the men's Final Four tournament in Indianapolis, said it had serious concerns about the law. By January 2016, Indiana had lost out on at least $60 million because of boycotts and refusal to run events or do business in the state.[5]

Many businesses and organizations announced that they would halt plans to do business or expand businesses in the state if Indiana did not repeal this law. Eventually, pressure from influencers effected change. The law was revised to specify that the

> religious freedom law cannot be used as a legal defense to discriminate against patrons based on their sexual orientation or gender identity . . . businesses or individuals [cannot] refuse to offer or provide its services, facilities, goods or public accommodation to any member of the public based on sexual orientation or gender identity, in addition to race, color, religion, ancestry, age, national origin, disability, sex or military service.[6]

Benioff, who we just mentioned, was one of the most vocal and visible leaders in this protest—said in a *Wall Street Journal* interview, "The next generation of CEOs must advocate for all stakeholders—employees, customers, community, the environment, everybody, not just for shareholders." Investors aren't upset with Benioff—and how could they be, with the company's stock soaring ninefold in the last ten years? Benioff makes giving back a core part of this business. He spends time in Hawaii, and he recently housed thirty Buddhist monks while their leader, Thich Nhat Hanh, received medical care, paid for by Benioff.

A picture emerges of Benioff as a CEO focused on more than traditional business topics. He has become a prominent leader in the fight to close the gender pay gap in Silicon Valley as well as outside it. In the past, C-level executives generally focused on business alone, lobbying for laws that would allow them to grow and become more profitable. Many opted to stay out of human rights issues. However, modern CEOs understand that there is little separation between work and personal life. CEOs are now celebrities, followed by millions on social media, and they recognize that what is good for the world is also good for their reputation.

Starbucks CEO Howard Schultz, too, has taken on an activist role, advocating for tougher gun control. Schultz penned an open letter on the Starbucks website, in which he said:

> From the beginning, our vision at Starbucks has been to create a "third place" between home and work where people can come together to enjoy the peace and pleasure of coffee and community. Our values have always centered on building community rather than dividing people, and our stores exist to give every customer a safe and comfortable respite from the concerns of daily life.

He asks customers not to bring firearms into stores even in states where open carry laws allow people to carry guns (he specifies law enforcement personnel as exceptions).[7]

Both generation Z and millennials want to do business with companies that have a soul, companies that are aware of societal issues and care about their customers, their employees, and the community. The 2008–2009 financial crisis, triggered by the subprime mortgage fallout, is still a clear memory in our brains. Many of our parents and grandparents lost their life savings—they had their homes taken back by the bank or had to find jobs as grocery store clerks or Starbucks baristas at an age when they thought they'd be hanging out at home with their grandkids. Many people believe that banks escaped this economic tragedy unscathed, while customers and lower-level employees suffered. Millennials remember clearly the Enron scandal, brought to light in 2001. It wasn't long ago we saw the BP oil spill killing birds and wildlife, destroying the world's precious oceans.

Your customers and employees, those of younger generations especially, want to do business with companies that have a conscience. Of course, none of us is doing business in a bubble. Companies that make decisions that consider all the lives—human and animal—affected as well as the environment impact will ultimately be seen as more modern, especially by younger generations.

Social Responsibility and Customer Experience

Many companies have give-back programs that offer their employees time off to volunteer, match employee donations to major causes, or sponsor community education activities such as hackathons. While these are all positive pursuits for companies, before they invest in such programs, they should look at their diversity initiatives. If I go to a company's website—or even look at a photo of its board—and I see only one kind of face, I wonder why. Why is it that so many companies have executive leadership teams made up entirely of men? Or perhaps there is one woman, often the head of human resources. Why do so many companies have only Caucasians on their leadership teams? Organizations need to think seriously about the message they're sending to their customers with all-white male executive teams and all-white male boards.

If your board won't listen to anything but the numbers, tell them that female consumers make more than 85 percent of all purchasing decisions.[8] Women are more reward based, democratic, team based, and transformational—so it's no surprise that companies with at least one woman on the board outperformed others by 26 percent. Additionally, having a woman on the board is correlated with a 20 percent decrease in a company's chance of going bankrupt.[9]

A board that lacks diversity makes a company seem out of touch. Our society is more diverse than ever. If you go to your website and see that your executive team and board all look the same, you have a big problem. This is not purely a human resources problem—it is also a PR, marketing, and customer experience problem. A diverse group will bring diversity of thought to your business, and they will better represent both the people who work for your company and those your company serves. People tend to hire those who look like they do, so make sure that you put the right people in charge of the hiring decisions to prevent homogeneity of your leadership team.

Making Good Decisions for Our Planet

Every day, your company must make decisions—these decisions have to do with your hiring practices but also with your environmental footprint. Do you take the cheaper shortcut, or do you consider the full implications of all the decisions you make? While this book espouses the importance of a new era for the consumer—one in which we can easily make purchases from the comfort of our laptop or phone—there's a dark side of online shopping as well. The $350 billion e-commerce industry has doubled in the past five years, with Amazon setting the pace.

While many of us love to hear our doorbells ring to signal a package left outside the house, truck deliveries take their toll on the air quality. The emissions from delivery trucks circling neighborhoods has raised emissions. A recent study explored the environmental effect of Internet shopping in Newark, Delaware, and found that a rise in e-commerce in recent years by local residents corresponded to an increase in greenhouse emissions—after all, many more trucks are on the road. Ardeshi Faghri, a professor of civil engineering at the University of Delaware, said the increase in various emissions—which he estimated at 20 percent from 2001 to 2011—"could be due to a multitude of reasons, but we think that online shopping and more delivery trucks are really one of the primary reasons."[10]

However, another study, cited in *Time* magazine, argues that delivery companies are more efficient at delivering items than you are at going out and buying them yourself. A study conducted in 2014 by researchers at the University of Washington found that use of a grocery delivery service can cut carbon dioxide emissions by at least half when compared with individual household trips to the store.[11] If companies deliver based on routes that cluster customers together, they can reduce CO_2 emissions by 80 to 90 percent compared to customers driving themselves.

One has to wonder if, in the future, the use of drones will address the problem of truck emissions. In a *60 Minutes* piece, Amazon CEO Jeff Bezos points out to interviewer Charlie Rose that drones will not only cut the diesel pollution produced by delivery trucks, but they will relieve congestion on crowded roads. But it's clearly not just truck emissions and road congestion that are concerning for the environment—it's all that packaging.

While consumers love the convenience of shopping on the web, the packaging necessary to shipping items safely creates a lot of waste from cardboard, Styrofoam, and bubble wrap. I recently moved into a house, and my husband and I ordered items like chairs from retailers. While I was very excited to see my new dining room furniture, I wasn't happy to unpack giant boxes filled with Styrofoam and more Styrofoam, some of it the kind that looks like curly cheese doodles.

According to an article in the *New York Times*, "E-Commerce: Convenience Built on a Mountain of Cardboard," in 2014 alone, 35.4 million tons of containerboard were produced in the United States, with e-commerce companies among the fastest-growing users. Companies like Amazon are aware of the problem. Since 2009, it has received 33 million comments, ratings, and photographs about its packaging as part of its "packaging feedback program." Amazon notes that it "used that feedback to make sure that cardboard box size was consistent with the size of the product." It also works with manufacturers to send some products without additional cardboard packaging.[12]

Doing Right by the Community

In one of 2015's most popular business books, *The Compass and the Nail: How the Patagonia Model of Loyalty Can Save Your Business, and Might Just Save the Planet*, author Craig Wilson talks about consumer choice. He says, "Reinventing and redesigning the fundamental relationships between providers of stuff and ourselves, the consumers of stuff, is our task; i.e., designing the Responsible Economy." Sustainable practices aren't just for baby boomers. Millennials, too, are highly concerned about the state of the Earth, and about where their stuff is made—and under what conditions.

Companies like Warby Parker use consumerism to give something to those in need. Warby Parker sells prescription eyeglasses, but instead of having customers come into a store, they will send them five pairs to try for five days. Customers buy the pair they want and send the rest back. Additionally, its website says,

> We believe that buying glasses should be easy and fun. It should leave you happy and good-looking, with money in your pocket. We also believe that everyone has the right to see. Almost one billion people worldwide lack access to glasses, which means that 15 percent of the world's population cannot effectively learn or work.

Warby Parker partners with a nonprofit to donate glasses to those who need them, and also trains people in the developing world to administer eye exams and sell glasses rather than giving glasses away.

Something else you, as a company, can do to be socially responsible is adjust your hiring practices to include those in underutilized demographics. Veterans, for example, often find it challenging to find jobs in the civilian work world. These candidates are disciplined and hard working, with a sense of responsibility you might not find in your recent college grads. Unfortunately, young veterans have higher unemployment rates than the population as a whole. It's a shame that men and women serve their country and, when finished, often can't find jobs.[13]

When staffing your contact center, you can also tap into the pool of stay-at-home moms and dads who are looking for remote work opportunities. Innovative technology designed to address contact center staffing gives you the opportunity to hire on-demand workers. This is of great help during busy times such as the holiday season or when you experience an unexpected lift in contact center volume. Staffing appropriately helps you avoid that unfriendly message to customers: "We are experiencing higher-than-normal call volume." This message means that the under-resourced and understaffed contact center has now become the customer's problem.

With proper resourcing, the company should never have to use the "higher-than-normal-call volume" message because the contact center will be able to staff up or down, according to volume. Staffing vendors can help with this, too. Through a vendor called WorkFlex solutions, you can hire on-demand agents who can drop and pick up shifts easily through the software. It's time to make customer-facing work a little more flexible. Additionally, if you're able to hire stay-at-home parents, they will be very grateful for the work.

***

Responsibility has to do with the way you treat your employees, your customers, and the broader community. When you hold yourself accountable to all of these stakeholders, business will get better. Companies that step outside the echo chamber and that consider the world around them will ultimately perform better. In the next chapter, we'll continue on this theme of sensitivity to global issues and trends by looking at disruption and innovation.

Notes

1. Jay Baer, *Hug Your Haters: How to Embrace Complaints and Keep Your Customers* (London: Penguin/Portfolio, 2013).
2. Shayla Price, "Why Customer-Focused Content Should Be a Priority," *Marketing Media Insider*, February 15, 2016, https://marketinginsidergroup.com/content-marketing/customer-focused-content-priority/.
3. Curtis M. Wong, "Indiana's Memories Pizza Reportedly Becomes First Business to Reject Catering Gay Weddings," *Huffington Post*, April 1, 2015, www.huffingtonpost.com/2015/04/01/indiana-pizza-gay-couples_n_6985208.html.
4. *Wikipedia*, s.v. "Religious_Freedom_Restoration_Act_(Indiana)," last modified November 17, 2016, https://en.wikipedia.org/wiki/Religious_Freedom_Restoration_Act_(Indiana)#cite_note-65.
5. Brian Slodysko, "Survey: Religious Objections Law Cost Indiana as Much as $60 Million," *The Chicago Tribune*, January 26, 2016, www.chicagotribune.com/news/local/breaking/ct-survey-religious-objections-law-cost-indiana-as-much-as-60-million-20160126-story.html.
6. Tony Cook, Tom LoBianco, and Doug Stanglin, "Indiana Governor Signs Amended 'Religious Freedom' Law," *USA Today*, April 2, 2015, www.usatoday.

com/story/news/nation/2015/04/02/indiana-religious-freedom-law-deal-gay-discrimination/70819106/.

7. Howard Schultz, "An Open Letter from Howard Schultz, CEO of Starbucks Coffee Company," *Starbucks Corporation*, September 17, 2013, www.starbucks.com/blog/an-open-letter-from-howard-schultz/1268.

8. Julie Hyman, "Women Make up 85% of All Consumer Purchases," *Bloomberg*, July 22, 2016, www.bloomberg.com/news/videos/b/9e28517f-8de1-4e59-bcda-ce536aa50bd6.

9. Jacob Morgan, "Why the Future of Our Organizations Depends on Having More Women in Management," *Forbes*, February 18, 2015, www.forbes.com/sites/jacobmorgan/2015/02/18/why-the-future-of-our-organizations-depends-on-having-more-women-in-management/#1502abe266a8.

10. Jamshid Laghaei, Ardeshir Faghri, and Mingxin Li, "Impacts of Home Shopping on Vehicle Operations and Greenhouse Gas Emissions: Multi-Year Regional Study," *International Journal of Sustainable Development & World Ecology* 23, no. 5 (2015): 381–391, doi:10.1080/13504509.2015.1124471.

11. Michelle Ma, "Grocery Delivery Service Is Greener Than Driving to the Store," *University of Washington Today*, April 29, 2013, www.washington.edu/news/2013/04/29/grocery-delivery-service-is-greener-than-driving-to-the-store/.

12. Matt Richtel, "E-Commerce: Convenience Built on a Mountain of Cardboard," *The New York Times Company*, February 16, 2016, www.nytimes.com/2016/02/16/science/recycling-cardboard-online-shopping-environment.html.

13. Lisa Rein, "Veteran Preference in Federal Hiring: The 'Third Rail of Civil Service Reform,' Expert Says," *The Washington Post*, June 27, 2016, www.washingtonpost.com/news/powerpost/wp/2016/06/27/veteran-preference-in-federal-hiring-the-third-rail-of-civil-service-reform-expert-says.

CHAPTER 10

Embrace Disruption and Innovation

What is the true meaning of innovation or disruption in terms of customer experience? In the past, industry experts and authors have proposed their own ideas around disruption. James Gilmore and Joseph Pine, in their 1999 book *The Experience Economy*, wrote that there should be drama (in terms of storytelling) when it comes to customer experience. They write that the customer experience should demand a stage, and the greater the length of time you've captivated your audience, the more success you've had with those customers. Time is valuable, the authors argue, and therefore you should aim to get the maximum time out of the customer.

Here's the problem with that approach: in most cases, customers want to spend as little time with you as possible. And that's normal. Doing business always involves some kind of transaction. When consumers conduct business with your company, they are doing so because you're fulfilling one of their needs. In some industries, customers may want to spend more time with a company—in the hospitality, travel, or entertainment arenas, for example. The customer "experience," as described by Gilmore and Pine, makes sense when it comes to a few experience-driven industries.

For example, many people in the Bay Area, where I live, are experience seekers. They enjoy wine tasting in Napa Valley, boating on Lake Tahoe, and participating in the annual Burning Man festival, a party in the desert that attracts techies, celebrities, and everyone in between. In fact, over the past fifteen years, adventure seeking has gotten a lot easier, thanks to the Internet.

You can easily book a niche experience from the comfort of your home via your phone or desktop. No longer do you have to rely on a travel agent to arrange an exotic trip—consumers learn everything they want to know from sites like Trip Advisor or Yelp. These are experiences where customers enjoy spending a lot of time—they're there to marinate in an experience, get distracted, and have fun. But this premise doesn't apply to all businesses across all industries. Most customers don't want to spend that much time with you. They simply want to achieve something with your product or service.

Do customers today have time for the distractions they know will greet them as they try to get their errands done? Most customers aren't looking to attend Burning Man when they do business with a company. While some customers seek these alternative experiences, featuring alternative experiences as an attraction at a retail store will not save the company. Most customers are looking for convenience—they want to do business with companies that make their lives easier. It's that simple.

For the past few years, the press has been obsessed with the idea of the "experience store." These are physical environments in which customers can interact with products. But in the future I don't believe customers will want to spend extended personal time with every product or service they are considering buying. The proof is in the numbers—customers are not visiting physical stores anymore. Amazon Prime set unbelievable expectations for customers, and services such as Instacart, Postmates, and now even Uber deliver food and make life more convenient for busy customers. While in the past digital and mobile platforms were an afterthought in retail business, we're approaching a time when physical retail space will be the afterthought. It's not a critical piece of a product strategy. Innovation or disruption in customer experience has to address the process, operations, and delivery of the product or service.

In today's economy, there is no way to avoid change and still succeed. Entire industries are blooming or dying overnight. If you bury your head in the sand, your company will likely be the next Blockbuster, unable to see change on the horizon. As author and CEO Michael Docherty writes in his book *Collective Disruption: How Corporations & Startups Can Co-Create Transformative New Businesses,*

The consumer marketplace has become a faster and more demanding game. Consumer products have to be better. Everyone—across all industries—is held to the highest standard. If in the old days customers might be satisfied with a mediocre product because that's all they knew to be available, today that veil is lifted.

Consider the following image that captures a three-horizon framework for sustained growth.[1]

Growth Horizons

The three-horizon framework was originally introduced almost twenty years ago in *The Alchemy of Growth: Practical Insights for Building the Enduring Enterprise*, but it maintains relevance today. Docherty provides an updated version of this framework in *Collective Disruption*, explaining that in today's hyperconnected and intensely competitive market, defending and refreshing the core in Horizon 1 is no longer enough to grow your business. Innovation here is what it takes to stay in the game.

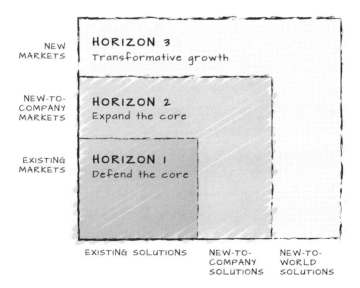

Figure 10.1 *Growth Horizons*

Most mature companies—especially those that are stagnating—are spending all of their time on Horizon 1, and eventually this strategy will kill them. Most companies, according to Docherty, reward managers who optimize business. Horizon 1 is about order and efficiency. There's no denying that this is important to success in the near term. However, in the long term, playing it safe by focusing only on your existing core solutions means obsolescence. It's too easy for products and services to be replicated. Businesses must look beyond their existing solutions and existing markets.

Horizon 2 is where companies focus on expanding their core and adding adjacencies. Earlier in the book, I talked about the Fulfillment by Amazon (FBA) program, which takes care of all aspects of its clients' e-commerce business, and this is an excellent example of a company exploring Horizon 2. Identifying adjacent opportunities becomes more important as you look for ways to grow your company. That said, you must simultaneously maintain your core.

Horizon 3 entails more breakthrough or transformative innovation. The gains are long term, not short, but the future of your company depends upon them. Companies tend to ignore this horizon because it demands more risk taking and may also require you to disrupt your business model—something most companies do not want to do and are not good at. While the ratios will vary depending upon your industry and situation, companies need to be spending, on average, about 70 percent of their energy on core activities, 20 percent on adjacent ones, and 10 percent on transformative activities. This is the ratio used by innovative companies like Google. The bigger a company gets, the harder it is for the company to embrace disruption and breakthrough innovation. But it's possible. In 2016, Facebook was ranked the second most innovative company by *Fast Company* for this very reason: it has not let its size get in the way of continuing to innovate, of acting like a start-up.[2]

One smart thing established companies can do is draw from the energy of start-ups and entrepreneurs to innovate their own business models. Start-ups need the support of the bigger company's capital and resources, and big companies need the infusion of fresh ideas from start-ups. Big companies can teach start-ups and entrepreneurs branding, scalability, business process, and much more.[3]

Today's blockbuster ideas are not coming from within the company. We see them generated by friends and family and posted to Kickstarter, or they involve handmade or vintage products listed on Etsy or eBay. Consider the story of Sophia Amoruso, who started her company Nasty Gal in 2006 by posting clothing she found in thrift stores or other vintage shops to eBay. Amoruso took photos of herself in the fashions and posted them to eBay—she resold a Chanel jacket for $1,000 she'd purchased at a Salvation Army store for $8. Amoruso turned Nasty Gal into a competitive retailer for young women, and gained 550,000 customers in more than sixty countries. In 2015, the retailer passed $300 million in revenue, tripling its sales in three years. Unfortunately, the company has hit some tumultuous times, and in late 2016 filed for Chapter 11, which will allow the company to reorganize. A statement from the company's current chief executive, Sheree Waterson, said, "We expect to maintain our high level of customer service and emerge stronger and even better able to deliver the product and experience that our customers expect and that we take pride in bringing to market."[4]

Amoruso, author of the book *#Girlboss*, is a thirty-two-year-old who *Forbes* listed in 2016 as one of the richest self-made women. Why would someone like Amoruso want to work for a big company when she could achieve much more with her scrappy, do-it-yourself attitude? Part of "doing more" is embracing disruption, not only to generate ideas for your products, but to attract talent to your company and keep them there. Many people who enter big companies to improve or change them eventually become disillusioned by the layers of bureaucracy and red tape. It's hard for most people to stomach.[5] But Amoruso's story also underlines that those who are adept at innovating and thinking about service from the customer's perspective may face challenges in running the company once it passes a certain level of complexity—a leader must maintain the commitment to the customer experience that launched her company's success, while also navigating successfully the intricacies of managing a large corporation.

There is no way, and I mean no way, for a company to embrace disruption without talking to customers on a frequent basis—once a year is simply not enough. Employees must be talking with customers all the time, and not just those who are easy to reach. Surveys on your community platforms and in other venues won't cut it. Your best ideas will come from your customers. They will also come from the people who spend the most time with your customers—if you are the CEO, I recommend that you get in front of both your customers and those with the closest proximity to your customers, your frontline employees.

The Changing Role of the Retail Store

The worldwide web and mobile have completely changed the game. Every week, we read about another retailer that has closed its doors, after failing to see the changes on the horizon. Remember Kodak? The company actually had digital camera technology in 1975, the first of its kind, but it thought the technology would compete with its photographic film business. Kodak clearly couldn't see the forest through the trees. We are all watching as Sears Holdings slowly dies. In an article from TheStreet.com, titled "20 Reasons Why Sears Is the Worst Stock in the World," the author writes,

> From an investing standpoint, the worst stock in the world is often so because the underlying company is the worst. It's an entity where, based on the financial statement trends and a common-sense take on future prospects, one wonders how the stock continues to be traded on public markets.[6]

When a large retailer goes out of business, most of us think to ourselves, "Yeah, I'm not surprised about that one." For a company like Sports Authority— another retailer taking a nosedive—the decline is attributable to poor running of the company, little or no attention paid to innovation, and a lack of oversight of the customer experience. Some retailers seem to have no idea that the Internet exists at all. Today, the lack of a web presence—or a half-baked presence—is a death wish, and it signals that a demise will come soon.

It's no secret that traditional retail companies are battling extreme competition from online retailers. Customers go into a brick-and-mortar store and immediately pull out their phones to compare products and pricing. To fight this trend, such stores can provide an experience that people can't get online. Ideally, the store experience elegantly supplements the offline platform, and vice versa. If you lead a traditional retailer and haven't started this reciprocal model, it's going to take a lot of effort and a big restructuring to put it in place, but the investment will be worth it. As I mentioned, the main attraction for your brand cannot be the in-store experience. If you don't have a digital and mobile component to what you offer, you likely will not be around in the next few years. However, you can match the work you're doing to engage and wow customers online with offline components that customers cannot get in virtual stores.

Disruption is about embracing the new *and* the old. Let's look at Sephora as an example. In the beauty category, it's difficult to get a sense of a product unless you can try it. At Sephora, you can usually find a beauty advisor who will recommend colors that match your skin tone and help you sample them. Every time I walk into Sephora, a sales associate asks me right away if I need help. Often, I take the associate up on the offer, and end up walking out of the store with products I didn't know I needed. It's a mix of education and special treatment—after all, who doesn't want her makeup done?

Sephora holds beauty workshops at certain locations, and there customers can get a lesson from an instructor. They can watch a tutorial on how to do their hair, nails, and makeup. There's a touchscreen kiosk that allows customers to find the right concealer, foundation, and lipstick for their skin tone. Additionally, on your computer desktop, phone, or tablet, you can test out Visual Artist, an augmented reality app that captures your face and, in real time, allows you to try on various shades of lipstick and eye shadow. Sephora knows its customers want to play with different looks, get educated about beauty products, and learn new tricks, and both its online and offline components meet these customer needs.[7]

Another example of the changing role of the retail store comes from Microsoft. I recently interviewed James Staten, chief strategist for Microsoft Cloud. Brick-and-mortar stores can compete with online retailers by leveraging emerging technologies to provide the most elegant, tailored, and luxurious experience possible. Imagine this: a customer walks into a store, and video cameras identify the customer. A CRM tells the employee working in the retail store who that customer is, his purchase history, and any additional information that would help the frontline worker suggest items tailored to what that customer might be interested in. Today, brands have access to facial recognition technology that would greatly improve the retailer's ability to provide a tailored experience.

Digital start-ups have clearly been inspired by the retail stores they are putting out of business. For example, Stitch Fix—a company I'll talk about again a little later in the book—offers personal styling. Its stylists send you items chosen specifically for your body type and style, and you purchase what you want from the box. Companies can only differentiate today by offering products and experiences that customers can't get anywhere else. Stitch Fix offers yet another example of a companies that thrives on customers seeking more tailored experiences. Retail—as we knew it—is no longer enough for the modern customer. Retailers need to create something special.

Pop-up shops are an increasingly good option for retailers that want to create some excitement. Here are some reasons to set up a pop-up store: testing a new revenue stream, engaging customers offline, creating "get it while it lasts" urgency, marketing merchandise themed around a holiday or season, educating new customers, setting up shop in a retail location where your customers are, and providing an experience that will eventually drive customers to your online presence.[8]

Other examples of companies that are expanding their store experiences are yoga apparel company Lululemon, which sponsors running clubs that let runners meet to enjoy a workout together, and Michaels, the chain arts and crafts supply store, where you can choose from online or offline classes and learn to knit, crochet, paint, draw, make jewelry, craft with paper, decorate cakes, and more. You can also throw a themed birthday party at Michael's for your kids. Another great example comes from the Amazon Smart Home team we talked about earlier in the book. Amazon offers free education for its prospects and customers. In exchange for this complimentary service Amazon builds stronger relationships with its community that it can later up-sell for complimentary products and services. Providing value through education—and building a relationship around that value provided—is key. These are not the major draws of these companies, however they build a community that ties the offline with the online. A company that embraces disruption marries offline and online experiences.

Case Study: Food52 Builds a Community With Content

Part of the disruption game is based on communication. How are you communicating with your customers? You cannot do what you've always done; you must do more to become a trusted advisor to your customers. Today's hottest brands are earning eyeballs by educating or entertaining customers, whether they're doing it themselves or partnering with a content provider to do so.

Today, the best companies spend time thinking about how to add value to their customers' lives through education and knowledge. They are thinking about how their customers can get the most value out of their products. Smart companies spend more of their time educating their customers and building relationships with their customers than they do on anything else. Food52, one company that focuses on education and relationship building, brings millions of people together by giving them a curated selection of recipes, content, and products for their kitchen and home. Food52 is not just a food blog. *Fortune* magazine published an article on Food52 saying,

> Food52 goes full circle. The content integrates the recipes, the recipes integrate the store, and the store's inventory is integrated into Collections, a Pinterest-like part of the site that lets users save recipes, articles, and items for purchase in one place.[9]

Fortune recognized the genius of Food52 by discussing the ways it works to prevent having the rug pulled out from under it by Amazon. The site sells authentic products that can be found only on Food52's website—these include hand-blown glass ice buckets, an exclusive spice blend of black sesame, ocean salt, and seaweed, and coffee travel kits, as well as wreaths. *Fortune* reports that Food52's "boutique appeal, bolstered by unusual content and a genuinely engaged audience, seems to be valuable as the digital media landscape becomes increasingly fragmented." The article's author applauds the company for going deep with its business strategy rather than far and wide. Food52, a pioneer successfully marrying content, community, and commerce, is the store of the future.

The company's numbers are strong: it has 5 million unique visitors monthly, 1 million registered users, 1.25 million e-mail subscribers, 2.5 million social media followers, and 90,000 shoppers (shop sales make up 60 percent of the company's overall revenue). Forty percent of Food52's audience is made up of the coveted millennial demographic.

In a few years, the company has ballooned to fifty-five full-time employees. In an article in the *Wall Street Journal*, "How Food52 Quadrupled Its Instagram Following in Less Than a Year," the site is recognized for earning 1.3 million followers in a short amount of time with video content, stunning food photography, and regrams (Instagram photos posted from other users). Food52 has almost one million Facebook fans and nearly half a million Twitter followers, and the company is also active on Snapchat. When I interviewed CEO and cofounder Merrill Stubbs, she talked about the importance of engaging with fans on Facebook, even in the comments section.[10]

Food52 is highly unique in that it publishes content, sells its own products, and also brings in ad revenue from brands. For example, according to the *Wall Street Journal*, Food52's most-liked Instagram photo to date is a shot of a pie with a diagonal lattice pattern sponsored by Simply Organic Foods. Not only is its social media presence powerful, but the company has a customer service team that supports the online store. In the spirit of "doing more," these agents are trained to answer questions related to pretty much anything in the Food52 sphere, whether it's a query about an actual cooking product ordered, how the website works, or a recipe posted.

Food52 is an industry-leading food destination flourishing in a very crowded marketplace. In fact, the world of online food blogs and websites is one of the most saturated on the web. So how does Food52 do it? With fanatical attention to quality content. The engagement factor is also key. Stubbs said,

> We're very happy if you come to the site for the first time and make a purchase but we're just as interested in converting you into a reader after that as we are in converting you to make a second purchase. We're not targeting a specific demographic. We want to build lasting lifelong relationships with people. We feel we can do that by providing them with what they need at any given moment and not forcing them down one path.

In my interview with Stubbs, she told me her company has a 99 percent approval rating for her customer service team, and she knows that because the company sends out surveys after every single interaction: "You don't want one person who can only answer questions about products because you might have someone calling in about something they ordered, or someone might call in and ask about a recent recipe featuring watermelon."

On-Demand Is On Point When It Comes to Content

Another prime example of innovation comes from an on-demand alcohol company called Thirstie that was launched in 2013. Thirstie has built a large following through its blog, called *The Craft*, which features more than forty pieces of content a month, generating 100,000 unique visitors per month. The company's numbers are strong, with 20 percent month-over-month sales growth.

In recent years, consumers enjoy being connoisseurs of liquor, and a new title has emerged: mixologist. Today, consumers enjoy making at home cocktails that mirror the complexity one might find in hip bars in cities like New York, San Francisco, and Chicago. More than 70 percent of *The Craft's* readers are millennials. The online magazine, which features recipes, interviews, and more, is hosted on the website Thirstie.com. Not only would you visit the company website to order a bottle of liquor delivered in less than an hour, but you might also find a recipe to impress your friends at the dinner party you're throwing. After Thirstie launched its blog, time on the website went from twenty seconds to six minutes. Eighty percent of the company's customers come in through editorial content.

Another interesting and unique aspect is shoppable pages within the content. This feature enables readers to make a purchase mid-article, without ever leaving the page. Founder and CEO Devaraj Southworth told me in an interview, "Imagine the ability to convert a reader into a buyer when purchase intent is the highest; it's valuable to the consumer and retailer, as well as the brand."

Thirstie was receiving 100 e-mails per month from people who were consuming its content via digital magazine and in-app recipes, but the one-hour delivery service wasn't available in the cities of these readers. The brand started offering rare and hard-to-acquire products delivered in two to three days. Thirstie is targeting a different customer with this venture, someone who is slightly older and is okay with waiting for a rare product. Southworth says this segment of the business generates a higher revenue per user, and the company makes more money when it facilitates the sale of a $200 bottle rather than a $20 bottle. He sees the opportunity in what he calls "lower operating pressures" with the longer delivery time.

Southworth explains that "Thirstie believes in educating the consumer at the right time and the right place. For example, a trendy Australian mixologist currently working in New York City might guest post on Thirstie's blog *The Craft*." Thirstie delivers all the ingredients readers need to replicate the cocktail recipe from that mixologist. Adding recipes to its app increased engagement by 70 percent.

***

These examples of companies on the cutting edge of customer experience should jog your brain around disruption and innovation. To be a company that does more, you must embrace changing business models. Companies that offer content-focused engagement strategies and tailored offerings for customers are all competing with innovation. Your company can learn from these agile brands as you assess your own customer engagement efforts. Compelling content must be an integral part of your customer engagement strategy.

Notes

1. John Rossman, *The Amazon Way: 14 Leadership Principles behind the World's Most Disruptive Company* (CreateSpace Independent Publishing Platform, 2014).
2. "Most Innovative Companies," *Fast Company*, November 20, 2016, www.fastcompany.com/most-innovative-companies.
3. Michael Docherty, *Collective Disruption*, 1st ed. (Boca Raton, FL: Polarity Press, 2015).
4. Samantha Masungaga, "Nasty Gal Files for Chapter 11 Bankruptcy Protection," *Los Angeles Times*, November 10, 2016, www.latimes.com/business/la-fi-nasty-gal-bankruptcy-20161110-story.html.
5. Clare O'Connor, "Nasty Gal's Sophia Amoruso Hits Richest Self-Made Women List with $280 Million Fortune," *Forbes*, June 1, 2016, www.forbes.com/sites/clareoconnor/2016/06/01/nasty-gal-sophia-amoruso-richest-women-net-worth/#65290a9044e1.
6. Brian Sozzi, "20 Reasons Why Sears Is the Worst Stock in the World," *The Street*, February 2, 2016, www.thestreet.com/story/13444692/1/20-reasons-why-sears-is-the-worst-stock-in-the-world.html.
7. Dan Tynan, "Sephora, Neiman Marcus Turn to In-Store Technology to Enhance the Retail Experience," *Biz Tech*, June 2, 2016, www.biztechmagazine.com/article/2016/06/sephora-neiman-marcus-turn-store-technology-enhance-retail-experience.
8. Humayun Khan, "Why Run a Pop-Up?" *Shopify*, November 21, 2016, www.shopify.com/guides/ultimate-guide-to-pop-up-shops/why-run-a-pop-up.
9. Erin Griffith, "Content, Commerce, and Cooking: How Food52 Is Making Small Community into a Big Business," *Fortune*, August 7, 2014, http://fortune.com/2014/08/07/content-commerce-cooking-food52/.
10. Mike Shields, "How Food52 Quadrupled Its Instagram Following in a Year," *The Wall Street Journal*, December 21, 2015, www.wsj.com/articles/how-food52-quadrupled-its-instagram-following-in-a-year-1450755231.

PART 3

Designing the Customer Experience of Tomorrow

In part 1, we looked at the current state of customer experience. For example, why is listening so hard for brands? We talked about how customers want to do business on their terms, and looked at how innovation in messaging apps is allowing them to do that. We talked about the role technology plays in customer experience and talked about how big data—if leveraged correctly—can empower brands to do more. In part 2, we explored the "do more" concept and discussed the role innovation has in creating knock-your-socks-off customer experiences. In part 3, we bring it all together by talking about how to actually design the customer experience of tomorrow. We do this by discussing the role of hiring and employee engagement. Additionally, we will look at generational customer experience and close by talking about how motivations matter.

CHAPTER 11

The Six Rings of the Modern Customer Experience

Unmemorable customer experiences are the fastest way for companies to make themselves obsolete. Every CEO today should communicate to employees that they should treat customers the same way they would treat guests in their homes. Not surprisingly, this customer strategy is preferred over one in which customers are treated like unwanted annoyances.

The truth is, if your products don't break easily, your service is above average, and if you are generally easy to do business with, you are light years ahead of your competition. It's really not that hard to differentiate. You know why? Most brands don't value the actual experience of the customer—so if you do, you are immediately differentiating your company from the others.

Simply put, you need to be easy to do business with. It takes a lot of effort to make something easy to use or to understand. In fact, the easier it is for a customer to do business with you, the harder your company probably had to work to build that experience. Uncomplicating the experience for your customer can be challenging for your company, but it's worth it when your customers tell everyone they know about your service.

Customer Experience Defined by the Experts

The phrase "customer experience" is a bit like a snowflake: no two definitions are alike. We'll start with our definition by looking to industry veteran John Goodman, author of *Customer Experience 3.0*, who conducted the first White House–commissioned study on customer service in the 1970s, defines customer experience as "end to end, ranging from honesty in marketing through the product lasting beyond the warranty period." He recognizes that customer experience does not equal customer service. It starts with the way you talk about the product, how you build the product, and it extends beyond the sale of the product.[1]

Managing Customer Perception

Hilton Worldwide has thirteen brands, spanning more than 4,660 hotels in more than 100 countries and territories. Scaling and streamlining customer experience at that level is no easy task. Mark Weinstein, SVP and global head of customer engagement, loyalty, and partnerships for Hilton Worldwide told me in a phone interview,

> It's not a singular customer experience—it's a series of interactions that are personalized, relevant, repeatable, and sustainable that create an essence or aura of your brand. Customer experience is not a happy coincidence. You wouldn't wing it when it comes to legal, finance, or accounting so why would you do that with customer experience?

Weinstein believes customer experience is judged by the customer and defined by Hilton as well. Meaning, Hilton is building the experience for the customer and, in creating that experience, is defining it for the customer. Hilton is influencing the perception of its customers. Weinstein said, "Some of it is reality and most of it is perception." He frequently asks his team, "How does our brand best serve our customers?" His role is to put mechanisms in place to streamline the digital and physical experiences on the customer side, so the customer can experience the brand "as we know they want to engage with us."

The Feeling Customers Get From Your Brand

At the time they were established, companies such as Mary Kay and Avon revolutionized the idea of customer acquisition and engagement—they enabled women to engage in direct-selling opportunities and build businesses out of their home. Avon was founded in 1886 and is now a $10 billion company.[2] Now, when the web is creating more distance between companies and customers, one company is tapping into networks, relying on the community of its local sellers to expand its business. I'm referring to the Stella & Dot family of brands, which relies on its sellers to spread the message through word of mouth and host parties to sell Stella & Dot jewelry and accessories.

Stella & Dot founder and CEO Jessica Herrin is a serial entrepreneur. She started the company known to many as WeddingChannel.com, the first company to put wedding registries on the web (it was sold to The Knot in 2006). As it was mentioned before, Herrin recently appeared on the television show *Undercover Boss* to take a look inside her own company. She told me she defines customer experience as

the feeling that customers get from your brand, your product, your services, that define whether or not it was a winning value exchange. Whatever dollars they took out of their product they got something more in return. It's the gratitude for every customer transaction. As a mission-driven company, we focus on the dollars earned by our field and flexible income. Every time someone shops with us, that is benefitting an independent business owner. We're grateful for anyone that shops with us and we want to deserve it.

Helping Customers Achieve Their Goals

David Edelman, partner in the marketing and sales practice for McKinsey, looks at customer experience from an operational view. He told me in an interview that he defines customer experience as "how the journey flows for a customer who wants to get something done. That could be the act of buying something, using something, or learning something. It can be getting entertainment out of something. It's all around the customer's goals." The customer's goals are the very reason the company exists. How is every department working to solve a problem for a customer, meet a customer's needs, and help him achieve a goal? Perhaps those questions are the reason Simon Sinek's book *Start with Why* resonated so much with the business community. Most employees don't think about why they do what they do. They go to work, do a job, and don't think about why they're there. The company would benefit from getting its managers in front of employees more to ensure that all team members know their purpose at work.

Edelman said,

> It's about how an organization delivers to the customer the ability to get something done. Marketing takes a heavy-handed approach to the journey revolved around learning, purchasing, and staying engaged in the brand. Customer service and operations are more involved in journeys about fulfilling the product and delivering service.

One challenge for companies is making sure that all the internal departments are collaborating around the customer, coming together to discuss the customer journey. All too often, marketing has no clue what customer support does. Marketing will send out promotions, and customer service only hears about the campaign when there is a flood of comments on the company's social media platforms.

Edelman added,

> Marketing, overall, is looking at all of the journeys to make sure the brand is coming through, the experience is one that will advance the brand in the customer's eyes, the best information about the customer is being used in the journey, the channels are all working together, and altogether the customer experience is something that is going to

drive differentiation. It's about the customer and their goals, but also what is going to distinguish the brand.

Along the same lines, in a 2007 article in *Harvard Business Review* called "What Is Customer Experience?" Christopher Meyer and Andre Schwager define customer experience as encompassing "every aspect of a company's offering—the quality of customer care, of course, but also advertising, packaging, product and service features, ease of use, and reliability." Very few people give extensive thought to the way their separate decisions shape customer experience.

To help those who historically haven't given much thought to customer experience, I created a framework called "The Six Rings of the Modern Customer Experience."

At the heart of these six rings is the seamless experience, the core of the ideal customer experience today. In the second layer is the collaboration tool, which enables your many departments to collaborate around that ideal seamless experience for the customer. On the third ring is the CRM—this muscle is the giant database that holds all your customer information. The fourth layer is personalization, something most companies are still struggling with, perhaps because personalization has failed marketers. A popular example of failed personalization occurs when you look at a pair of shoes online, and then ads for those shoes follow you for weeks. Perhaps you already bought them, but they continue to follow you. Why would a company want to market you shoes you've already bought? Why wouldn't it show you a matching bag or dress instead?

The fifth ring in the frame are your channels. A modern customer experience allows customers to communicate with companies wherever it is most convenient for the customer rather than vice versa. As new channels grow in popularity, your team is already there, engaging with customers. You need to be fast and fearless in your ability to pivot with the times; as channels grow, you must be one of the first out of the gate. The sixth ring features your stakeholders. These are your customers, prospects, partners, influencers, and the general public.

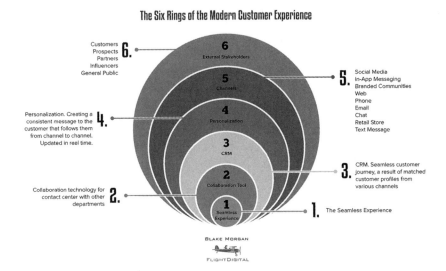

Figure 11.1 *The Six Rings of the Modern Customer Experience*

While these rings may not all seem highly significant to running a cohesive customer experience operation, they are. They all contribute extensively to your customer experience, and by leaving out a piece, you make yourself vulnerable. On the other hand, if you address the six rings shown in Figure 11.1, you will be light years ahead of others.

Yoga in Aisle Three

Today, most products and services look alike. Very few things out there are one of a kind. Joseph Pine and James Gilmore, authors of *The Experience Economy*, wrote, "Indeed, in a world saturated by largely undifferentiated goods and services the greatest opportunity for value creation resides in staging experiences."

The Experience Economy was groundbreaking at its 1999 publication, but it doesn't get to the heart of the customer experience crisis we are facing today. For example, a recent *Wall Street Journal* article, "Attention Shoppers: Yoga in Aisle 3," describes a handful of grocery chains that offer amenities ranging from cooking and exercise classes to peppermint foot scrubs, facial waxing, and bike repair. The article notes that supermarkets have had bank branches and dry cleaners in their stores for some time, but making them into village-like destinations is a new experiment. But I don't think it's enough. Most companies will not survive by simply creating something out of the ordinary in their retail locations. When I pick up my dry cleaning, I'm not looking to do a wine tasting or get a massage. I simply want my clothes returned to me cleaner than when I dropped them off.

Can you imagine if all brands try to be everything to everyone? Do most people want their grocery store to be their gym too? Customers prefer the convenience and speed of doing business on mobile and the Internet, but retail is still hanging on for dear life trying to transform itself into something else. Transforming retailers into experience centers will not be enough.

Today's grocery stores should focus on the problem they solve for people: feeding them. Grocers today have much competition; Amazon Fresh delivers groceries, and services such as Blue Apron and Gobble deliver neatly packaged ingredients so the consumer can make the meal themselves at home. These "un-made" meal delivery services offer convenience—not only can customers avoid the store, but they don't have to think up recipe ideas or estimate how much of each ingredient they will need. These tasty and healthy dishes can be made in less than thirty minutes. Users can choose their meals, which come with a story about the food and details the geographic region the meal comes from and why it became so popular. When I go to the grocery store, I mostly know what I'm buying, but it still takes me thirty minutes to get through the store. That's a lot of time, especially when you consider the driving, parking, and paying—and then you still have to go home and cook the dinner. And there are dishes to do too! Grocers need to think about what consumers in their local neighborhood are looking for and how consumer behavior is changing. Today, consumers may prefer not to go to the store at all. In the Bay Area, consumers seek local, organic ingredients, food that has a story behind it, and food that is healthy and made sustainably.

In the revised edition of *The Experience Economy* authors Gilmore and Pine describe how "countless chains have met their demise . . . as they insisted on merely merchandising finished goods." These stores are doing the bare minimum to keep their doors open. Today, it's not enough to merely sell a product—you need to do more for the customer than you did in the past. Gilmore and Pine discuss the value in "treating services as the stage and the goods as the props for staging engaging experiences."[3] Essentially, selling the product becomes an excuse to provide something memorable to the customer.

As hard as retailers try to do something extra to drive foot traffic to their retail locations, their efforts are not enough. One by one, big box retailers are being forced to close their doors. In 2016, more than 2,500 big box retail locations closed, including locations for Target, Walmart, Kmart, Sears, and more. These are stores set to close in 2016 and 2017: Wet Seal (more than 500 stores), Office Depot (400 stores), Barnes & Noble (223 stores), Walgreens (200 stores), Children's Place (200 stores), Aeropostale (175 stores), Walmart (154 stores), Finish Line (150 stores), American Eagle (150 stores), Sports Authority (140 stores), Macy's (40 stores), Gap/Gap Kids (35), Sears/Kmart (128), Chico's (120), Pier One, Sports Chalet (48), Target (13), and JC Penney (8).[4]

What are retailers to do when the cards are stacked against them? They must begin the process of business transformation. According to a recent article in *Harvard Business Review* called "What Do You Mean by Business Transformation?" there are three types of business transformation. The first type is *operational*, and it involves doing what you are currently doing, only doing it better, faster, or cheaper. The companies that are "going digital" fit into this category—they're solving old problems with new technology.

The second type of business transformation is *core transformation*. As a business, you're still doing what you've always done but in a different way. The third type of business transformation is *strategic*. It has the most possible benefit and also the most risk, because it requires the company to change its essence. Examples of companies engaged in this type of transformation include Apple, which went from making computers to designing gadgets; Google, which went from selling advertising to promoting self-driving cars; and even Amazon, which, as we talked about earlier, went from retail sales to cloud computing. It's not enough to offer yoga at the grocery store, or put a museum in your corporate headquarters. While that might intrigue some consumers, it does not yield the growth a business would get from strategic business transformation.[5]

Can you think of many purchases you've made in the last few weeks where the company staged an experience so good you're still thinking about it? Probably not! These experiences are still few and far between. The digital landscape represents both an opportunity and a big challenge, and it's the brand's responsibility to create something so easy it's stupid simple for the customer. Customers already have too much to worry about. They are going to flock to the services that make their lives easier.

Customer Effort Framework

"More is more" doesn't always mean talking more or spending more. It means some companies spend more focus, energy, and resources creating better experiences for their customers. Customers should not have to spend a lot of time or effort when they do business with your company. It should be incredibly easy to purchase a product, use it, and get help with it. In a survey of more than 75,000 consumers, the number-one most important factor in customers' loyalty is reducing the work they must do to get their problem solved.[6] Companies need to focus on making their processes easier on their customers, even if it makes work harder for themselves. In any line of work, if you care about quality, you work very hard to make your offerings and processes seem effortless.

In the framework below, you have on one side the attributes of companies that require low customer effort; these are the companies that earn loyalty by making things easier on their customers (and harder on themselves). They embrace a more-is-more philosophy.

The company that is "low effort" for its customers doesn't spam customers with massive amounts of irrelevant content. Instead, it provides personalized, just-in-time content that is relevant for the customer. This is the company that offers easy return policies; some even allow customers to borrow products and try them for a few days. The company that requires low

Figure 11.2 *Attributes of Company Effort*

effort for customers provides compelling self-service options. It has thought of every issue or question customers might have and has created an easy do-it-yourself solution for that issue. But this shining example of a "low-effort" company also makes it ever so easy to reach a person when one is needed. Instead of hiding behind clunky IVR technology, this company provides access to a person 24–7! When you do reach that agent, she doesn't rely on a script—she actually talks to you like you're a person. The entire experience is digital and mobile friendly for the customer, and the agent can easily see what the customer is doing through a CRM, making everything the agent says to the customer relevant and timely. This is not a company that burdens its customers with paper, or, even worse, sends communications in the mail! The horror! No, this company is completely digitally savvy, and the customer can easily reach service agents on any channel. This company will be in business for many years to come!

On the other side of the equation is the company that demands high effort from its customer. Unfortunately, this includes most of the world's businesses today. This high-customer-effort company makes life harder on customers and easier on itself. This is the company that creates mass marketing content and mass customer service content. It's a real stickler with returns—if items are not in perfect condition with tags attached (or packaging unopened) and returned within the short period of time allowed, the customer is stuck with the product. It's a defective product? Oh, well, sorry!

This company is making the customer sweat with complicated self-service options and outdated knowledge repositories. It offers the kind of self-help options that send customers to the self-help section of the bookstore. And if you need to talk to a customer service agent, this company has very long wait times; you are likely to hear the IVR tell you, "We are experiencing higher-than-normal call volume." This also means, "We've got some variation and we didn't plan for it—also, we don't want to spend the money to hire extra resources, so please hold the line while we continue to be frugal with our customers." When your turn to talk to the agent arrives, that person is speaking from a script! The person sounds like a robot. Transactions at this high-customer-effort company are still done on paper. A CRM? Forget it! These agents ask customers to repeat information at every turn. Finally, you expect to reach this company on a variety of channels? Forget about it! This company barely has its call center phone lines working. Everything about this company screams high customer effort, and it probably won't realize how awfully it treated customers until it's too late.

***

In this chapter, we talked about the six rings of the modern customer experience, we looked at the way customer experience is defined by the experts, and we talked about customer perception, the customer journey, and customer effort. We also looked at classic theories on customer experience and whether they apply today. In the next chapter, we'll look at the way your company's culture, vision, and priorities will shape your customer experience in the future.

Notes

1. John A. Goodman, *Customer Experience 3*, 1st ed. (New York: AMACOM, 2014).
2. *Wikipedia*, s.v. "Avon Products," last modified November 18, 2016, https://en.wikipedia.org/wiki/Avon_Products.
3. Pine, Joseph, Gilmore, James, 1999, *The Experience Economy*, p. 37, Edward Elgar Publishing Ltd, UK.
4. Alicia Adamczyk, "Sears, Walmart, Target & Others That Have or Will Close Stores in 2016," *Time*, April 22, 2016, http://time.com/money/4304622/stores-closing-in-2016/.
5. Scott Anthony, "What Do You Really Mean by Business 'Transformation'?" *Harvard Business Review*, February 29, 2016, https://hbr.org/2016/02/what-do-you-really-mean-by-business-transformation.
6. Matthew Dixon, Karen Freeman, and Nicholas Toman, "Stop Trying to Delight Your Customers," *Harvard Business Review*, July–August 2010, https://hbr.org/2016/02/what-do-you-really-mean-by-business-transformation.

CHAPTER 12

Culture, Vision, and Priorities

If you've ever worked with a company that has more than 100,000 employees, you know what a nightmare it is to get work accomplished when you may never be in the same time zone with some of your colleagues, let alone the same room. Such large companies have legacy cultures, bureaucracy, and many roadblocks to getting things done, particularly for the customer. When you want to create change, those who created the legacies you are challenging may be very uncomfortable. Most people would rather keep the status quo. When it comes to change management, there's no greater challenge than communication. Complicating that challenge is the reality that many pieces of the customer experience and the customer journey are often owned by different people—people who will never meet, and who don't even work in the same country.

The ugly truth is that many executives at big companies are barely treading water. They are already working overtime, stressed about being replaced by someone younger and with a lower salary. Most employees are stressed about their survival at the company, which often depends on who likes you and how much. Another ugly truth about the corporate world: getting stuff done is not necessarily a big predictor of success.

And just like many executives inside some of the world's biggest companies, many employees are barely treading water. Additionally, employees today are eager to move up—and they depend on the mentoring of leaders to be able to do that—but many leaders don't have the time.

Employees—especially millennials—are disengaged quickly when they see how few opportunities there often are to move up at big companies. In order to change the company's culture, you need to take a look at how your company is run, what the culture is, and how the employees feel about working there. But all too often, in today's environment, there simply isn't time.

When you work at a big company, you're dealing with a lot of politics. It is widely known that if you want to do well in your job and move up in the company, you would be wise to make your boss look good. You might also get promoted if someone influential likes you, if you get noticed for a project or program (often, one person gets credit for something many contributed to), if you remind someone at the top of themselves (yes, lack of diversity is a big problem in the corporate world), or if you follow directions and don't ask questions. While this may seem a cynical view of work, it's the reality in much of the corporate world.

So how does this corporate reality impact customer experience? It's the reason you were put on hold for twenty minutes with a call center (and were then hung up on), and the reason you had to repeat your information to your bank five times, and the reason no one responded to your tweet or Facebook post. Many parts of the customer experience are labeled as costs rather than investments, and bureaucracy is typically one of the main culprits when companies don't improve customer experience year after year. Who wants to stick their neck out for the customer when they're already worried their head is on the chopping block? It's 2017, and the tech sector is seeing some massive layoffs. No one wants to be next out the door. Employees have baby formula to buy, car and house payments to make, and a trip to Hawaii planned for one of their two sacred weeks off. Most employees try to keep their heads down and do what they're told—and what they're told is that change is bad.

A full quarter of employees don't trust their employer, according to a 2014 American Psychological Association survey of 1,562 U.S. workers.[1] Will a poor employee experience be the downfall of many of the Fortune 500 companies today? It's likely. The average tenure of companies in the S&P 500 has shrunk from sixty-one years in 1958 to just eighteen years as of 2012. At this rate, 75 percent of the current S&P 500 will be replaced by 2027. Having engaged employees matters.[2] Some companies are lucky enough to have brave employees who choose to champion the customer's plight. These highly patient, talented communicators know enough people in the company to actually get work done on behalf of the customer.

Customer-focused cultures tend to also have more employee-focused cultures. There's transparency about what the company will and won't stand for. Generally, these cultures thrive in smaller companies—and these companies are doing very well. An important factor in creating a customer-focused culture is leadership. When leaders are trained to be strong managers, they build stronger cultures. They know how to set an example, engage employees, and cut out the nonsense that is so prevalent in corporate life. According to a Deloitte study, high-performing companies spend one and a half to two times more on leadership training than other companies do, and they reap results that are triple or quadruple the levels of their competitors.[3]

Hiring Practices for Customer-Focused Teams

You know the classic interview question, "Can you share with me a time you had a challenge at work, and how you overcame that challenge?" People who work directly with customers are overcoming major challenges for customers every single day. They are in the "overcoming challenges" business. I believe that the best employees, whether their position is at the leadership level or the intern level, exude gratitude, patience, and empathy. The personalities, attitudes, and work styles of your employees have an immense effect on the customer experience. It's not just customer-facing employees who need to bring their best to work every day for the customer; all your employees, including those who work behind the scenes, have an impact on the customer experience. Below, I explore some traits to seek when hiring that will help you choose employees who put customers first.

Innate Curiosity

I recently interviewed Susan Ganeshan, CMO of software company Clar-abridge, who has been a CMO more than once. Over the span of her career, she's mentored and groomed four employees to help them become CMOs in their own right. Ganeshan knows the average tenure of a CMO is only eighteen months. When I asked her what she attributed her own success to, she said it was her curiosity. If she wanted to figure out how to solve a problem for her company, she simply picked up the phone and called someone to ask. People who are curious end up building better products, contributing more to the company, and are generally stronger problem solvers for the customer.

In an interview in the *Harvard Business Review*, Michael Dell, chief executive of computer company Dell, Inc., answered a question about how to succeed in turbulent times by saying he'd place "a bet on curiosity." In fact, many C-level executives believe in the power of curiosity. In a PwC survey of more than a thousand CEOs, a number of them cited "curiosity" and "open-mindedness" as leadership traits that are becoming increasingly critical in challenging times. It seems counterintuitive that both leaders and employees would benefit from asking questions rather than quietly solving problems on their own, but curiosity is the consistent underlying attribute of successful employees. The same *HBR* article cites *The Innovator's DNA*, in which authors Clayton Christensen, Hal Gregersen, and Jeff Dyer note that curious, questioning leaders overcome risk because they have a blend of humility and confidence:

> They were humble enough to acknowledge to themselves that they didn't have all the answers, and confident enough to be able to admit they don't have all the answers in front of everyone else. If you look back at business history, the most egregious mistakes were a result of employees not speaking up when something clearly wasn't right. One employee asking one question could have prevented some of the most costly mistakes in corporate history.[4]

Curiosity is a critical attribute of those taking up the role of the intrapreneur. A play on the word *entrepreneur*, intrapreneurs are employees but are given the freedom, resources, and encouragement to solve problems within the company. Companies that have intrapreneur programs include Pixar, AT&T, Cisco, Adobe, and General Mills. The companies that make intrapreneurship part of their competitive strategy encourage curiosity and questioning on the part of their employees.

Can-Do Attitude

Have you ever seen the show *Dirty Jobs* with Mike Rowe? Mike takes the audience into some of the toughest jobs in the world. Discovery Channel describes the show by saying

> Host and everyman Mike Rowe gets the grimy scoop on downright nasty, but vital, occupations in Dirty Jobs. Rowe could be processing smelly seafood in a fish factory, collecting bat guano for prized fertilizer or cleaning septic tanks to maintain a fresh-smelling environment. His apprenticeship never ends as he learns from those who keep our world running smoothly.[5]

Did you know that Rowe is also an opera singer? He performed with the Baltimore Opera before starting a career in television.[6]

I like Rowe for the example he sets: he's willing to do any type of job. In this day and age, you need to hire people who don't have a problem getting their hands dirty or doing things that aren't in their job description. Not only is this imperative for customer-facing roles, but for all roles within the company. While expecting everyone to have a "whistle while you work" attitude every single day might seem overly idealistic, it certainly doesn't hurt to hire people who appreciate the opportunity to work and aren't above doing the dirty jobs that come with running a business.

Good With Tech

I want to preface my statement here by saying that I do not know how to code, and I don't see myself in the near future taking a learn-to-code class, but

I wish I had acquired this skill when I was a kid. I believe it helps give your business a creative edge when your employees have at least cursory knowledge in a few different areas; for example, do they know some html? Can they easily fix a web page? Other valuable traits include navigating social media analytics without much fuss and drawing conclusions by organizing and analyzing data. Have you heard the word *Luddite*? The term Luddites describes workers who, in the years 1811 to 1816, destroyed machinery they saw as a threat to their jobs, and the definition has been expanded to refer to those who oppose or resist new technology. Technology will soon drive everything we do. If someone describes himself as a Luddite in a job interview, you won't want to hire him, even if the role is seemingly unrelated to technology.

Team-Oriented Attitude

In today's competitive job market, aligning a group of motivated individuals around a common goal can be challenging. After all, there are generally a limited number of roles at the top, and most people want to move up in their careers—especially millennials. Millennials are accused of having unrealistic expectations for how fast they will move up in the company. While strong motivation and a little competitiveness is not the worst thing in the world, if you create a culture of competition at your company, don't expect people to collaborate and share ideas.

You want to create a culture where employees are rewarded for lifting their team up rather than for being a solo performer. If you have a lot of employees who appear to be self-centered, you might be biased toward hiring people with a competitive personality, but you could also be encouraging self-interested behavior through the values your company espouses. If you hire smart people who have strong values, pay them well, and provide incentives that inspire collaboration, you will find your company is more productive overall.

Down-to-Earth Attitude

Every hiring suggestion I've touched on in this chapter upholds traits such as humility, hard work, and gratitude. In this book, I've mentioned a few examples of executives doing the work that their employees do to understand what it's like to actually be a frontline worker in their company. The first example was Jessica Herrin of Stella & Dot, who went undercover on *Undercover Boss* to perform various jobs such as customer service agent, jewelry maker, and sales rep; the second example was Brian Chesky, CEO of Airbnb, who himself hosts guests in his apartment.

Another example, one I haven't mentioned, is Luxe Valet, an innovative start-up out of the sharing economy. This service provides valet parking in select cities where parking is often difficult. Though parking duties are generally handled by frontline workers, the executives from Luxe Valet take time to park cars themselves on occasion, in order to understand the customer journey, and to see what life is like for employees as well. Every employee should be required to spend time doing various tasks within the company, so he or she can understand how the products and services are made and delivered. I believe that all employees would benefit from spending time in the contact center as well. People who are willing to dive in and contribute at any level show that they are not privileged and are happy to extract knowledge from at kinds of valuable experiences.

***

In this chapter, we've gone over the practices and challenges surrounding building competitive companies with sound hiring and engagement strategies. We've addressed the fact that companies cannot expect employees to behave in a way that managers don't. We talked about the value of humility, curiosity, and investing in leadership training. There is no way to get around investing in your people. The experiences your companies offer your customers will only be as compelling as the people who built them. If you want compelling customer experiences, start with looking at your people practices. In the next chapter, we'll look at generational customer experience, breaking down each group by looking at cultural factors, tastes, and customer preferences by age.

Notes

1. Andre Lavoie, "4 Reasons You Need to Embrace Transparency in the Workplace," *Entrepreneur*, April 28, 2015, www.entrepreneur.com/article/245461.

2. Minutemen, "Increasing Churn Rate in the S&P 500: What's the Lifespan of Your Stock?" *Seeking Alpha*, November 6, 2014, http://seekingalpha.com/article/2651195-increasing-churn-rate-in-the-s-and-p-500-whats-the-lifespan-of-your-stock.

3. David Brown, Veronica Melian, Marc Solow, Sonny Chheng, and Kathy Parker, "Culture and Engagement: The Naked Organization," *Deloitte University Press*, February 27, 2015, https://dupress.deloitte.com/dup-us-en/focus/human-capital-trends/2015/employee-engagement-culture-human-capital-trends-2015.html.

4. Warren Berger, "Why Curious People Are Destined for the C-Suite," *Harvard Business Review*, September 11, 2015, https://hbr.org/2015/09/why-curious-people-are-destined-for-the-c-suite.

5. "Discovery Channel's 2010–11 Upfront Slate is Filled with Epic Specials, Favorite Long-Run Series and Exciting New Talent," *Discovery*, April 8, 2010, https://corporate.discovery.com/discovery-newsroom/discovery-channels-2010–11-upfront-slate-is-filled/.

6. *Wikipedia*, s.v. "Mike Rowe," last modified November 11, 2016, https://en.wikipedia.org/wiki/Mike_Rowe.

CHAPTER 13

Generational Customer Experience

Here's the thing about generations: the statistics don't represent every single person, and there are always exceptions to the rule. Also, generations evolve in tandem with changes occurring in society. For example, I did not grow up with the Internet and did not have a cell phone until I was in college; however, that doesn't mean my expectations are much different from those of a young person who grew up with the Internet and a smartphone. I have become accustomed to the conveniences we enjoy today, and my expectations are in line with modern life. However, the technological landscape matters a lot, and it has a big impact on a generation's expectations, overall.

Generational studies are helpful because they show us a sampling of a group, and sometimes that sampling gives us good ideas about how the entire group behaves; but the studies are never 100 percent applicable to all people because they are based on just a selection. Many baby boomers are both better with and more involved with technology than some people of younger generations. Think about the baby boomer Ray Kurzweil, inventor, author, and technology genius, who has plans to cryogenically freeze himself when he dies. This is a baby boomer who fully embraces technology. That said, the environment a given generation grew up in affects their preferences and life choices. Although some generational statistics aren't representative of everyone in that demographic, they do still matter, and they can inform some of your decision making regarding customer strategy. Let's take a look at the four biggest generations who are adults or near-adults today.

Generation Z

Generation Z is the group born after 1995, though some argue that generation Z starts at the year 2000. According to *Forbes*, in 2015, generation Z made up 25 percent of the U.S. population, making it the biggest generation in U.S. history. Don't be fooled by older generations' portrayal of generation Z as technology-addicted zombies; this is a thoughtful, open-minded, responsible, and determined group.[1]

Contrary to popular belief, most members of generation Z prefer in-person interaction rather than online interaction, but, as you know, they love Snapchat and other tools that allow them to communicate privately with their friends and build relationships through direct or group messaging. Predominately the children of gen Xers, they are the least likely to believe in the American dream because they saw their older siblings in generation Y struggle with the job market. Generation Z were kids during the Great Recession, and some witnessed the September 11th terrorist attacks as very young children. According to *Business Insider*, generation Z is more conservative, money-oriented, entrepreneurial, and pragmatic about money, when compared with millennials.[2] Members of generation Z are against changing themselves to match someone else's idea of perfection—for example, they are not fans of photoshopping their pictures. How refreshing to have a generation that feels comfortable broadcasting themselves as they really are.

How Brands Can Build Customer Experiences for Generation Z

Generation Z is a generation armed with credit cards. Spending in this demographic will reach $200 billion by 2018. Additionally, they influence what mom and dad buy—9.7 percent of adults say their children influence 100 percent of what they buy, up from 7.6 percent in 2014.

And this is a device-dependent group: in 2015, 77 percent of twelve- to seventeen-year-old Americans owned a cell phone.[3] Generation Z lives on their phone, spending 15.4 hours on their smartphones per week, which is more time than they spend with any other device; they receive more than 3,000 texts per month. This generation spends an average of 15.4 hours per week on their phones.[4] Eighty-four percent of generation Z browse the web while watching TV, and 70 percent watch more than two hours of YouTube per day.[5] I visit some of the most popular YouTube channels, and I really don't understand the appeal of these self-made stars—but I give them credit: they must have something compelling to offer to generation Z or else they wouldn't have viewers.

Brands are engaging these YouTube megastars as brand ambassadors or signing them to advertising deals, but the industry is cooling off. Companies aren't hiring YouTube stars at the same rates they used to because the value isn't always there. Yet this market exists because generation Z is influenced by what's coming out of their screens—and the screen they pay attention to is their phone. You have to earn your engagement from generation Z by drawing them in a smart way, not by making assumptions about what they like. They respond to short-form visual marketing like edgy video. Consider posting videos to YouTube, Instagram, or even Snapchat.[6]

Generation Z are not fans of traditional advertising, and, when it comes to digital advertising, according to an article in *MediaPost*, "optimistic" analysts claim that apps that block advertising (which are gaining traction) represent "only" around $1 billion annually in lost revenue, but others predict that they could decimate the entire digital publishing industry.[7] The same *MediaPost* article reports that generation Z finds ways to avoid print media altogether. This generation watches TV content on a DVR, breezing right past advertising, or through a paid streaming service that has little or no advertising. Traditional advertising is going by the wayside as a result of consumer preference (most of us hate it), and content will likely look completely different in the near future. Consumers' ability to block advertising could indeed decimate digital publishing if the industry doesn't figure out another business model.

Generation Z likes storytelling and visual displays, and this generation enjoys being culture creators themselves. More than 25 percent of gen Zers post original video content on a weekly basis. That's one out of every four! The overarching trend to know with regard to generation Z? Don't rely on TV to reach them; instead, find ways to make your brand relevant to them through compelling storytelling, and deliver that content on the devices they prefer.

Millennials

Millennials are not extremely different from their younger siblings, the gen Zers. For example, millennials also value storytelling across multiple platforms. In the article "How Millennial Labels Are Bringing Brand Loyalty Back," retail consultant Robert Burke says,

> It's about creating a lifestyle and telling the story really well [across multiple platforms]. The customer today is more curious and better informed than ever before. It's not just enough for them to run out and buy, say, a ruffle top. They want to know everything about it: what it stands for, who's behind it, how it was made, and the type of person it represents.

Millennials also care about where the product was made. They want to be able to tell their friends the story of the product, if it should come up. According to the article, in the past, people might have identified with a particular brand, but when the world became more trend driven, labels didn't carry the same weight. Now, the pendulum appears to be shifting in favor of smaller brands.[8]

But millennials don't value ownership over experience as generations in the past did. They want to share experiences, and studies show they'd rather pay for an experience than a product. A study conducted by Harris Interactive found that millennials not only value experiences, but they are spending their time and money on them. The study reported that from concerts and social events to athletic pursuits, to cultural experiences and events of all kinds . . . for this group, happiness isn't as focused on possessions or career status. Living a meaningful, happy life is about creating, sharing, and capturing memories earned through experiences that span the spectrum of life's opportunities.[9]

Since 1987, the share of consumer spending on live experiences and events relative to total U.S. consumer spending increased 70 percent. Millennials and their little brothers and sisters are not interested in purchasing the same status items that their parents were. This generation embodies changing values about ownership—they prefer access over ownership—but that's not all that's changing. Millennials expect engagement back from the brand right away. Seventy-two percent of customers who complain on Twitter expect a response within one hour.[10] Even millennials who did not grow up with the Internet have become accustomed to instant gratification. I was in high school when instant messaging first came on the scene, and I can remember the thrill of getting an instant message (of digital text) back from someone on the other side of the screen. It was uncanny!

I did not grow up in an always-on world, but I can't say I mind it. Did the technology shape millennials? Or did millennials simply go out and build the technology that suited their desires, personalities, and tastes? It's likely it was the latter, as millennials like me did not grow up with instant gratification. Much of my generation sent college applications through snail mail. Generation Z will never know what it's like to get such important news about your future through the mail.

Amazon, Postmates (on-demand delivery), and Instacart (groceries delivered in an hour) have helped set a precedent of instant gratification by offering same-day delivery. Now, millennials enjoy having pretty much anything they want delivered right to their door. Every day, new companies pop up that allow millennials to spend less time shopping and more time doing other things they love. This generation is looking at new ways to simplify their lives, whether that means owning less stuff, renting rather than buying products (such as cars, houses or apartments, and even clothes), or even moving back in with mom and dad. According to Pew Research in 2014, for the first time in more than 130 years, adults ages eighteen to thirty-four were slightly more likely to be living in their parents' home than they were to be living with a spouse or partner in their own household.[11]

Life is not what it was for our parents' generation. In the 1970s and 1980s, if you were middle class and you wanted to buy a house—even in California—you went out and bought a house. In fact, my parents underbid on their house in Orange County, California, and they got it anyway. I live in the Bay Area, and anything on the market here easily goes for 20 to 30 percent above the already-steep asking price. In California, you have the perfect storm of too many people and not enough housing. But real estate ownership is no longer the symbol of accomplishment that it once was. According to a *Newsweek* article, "Why Millennials Still Move to Cities," millennials have put off having kids, and are instead using their twenties to focus on their careers and travel. They are in no rush to give up their freedom and tie themselves to kids and mortgage. Additionally, *Newsweek* talks about the innovation economy, recalling population moves to cities many decades ago because that is where factory jobs were plenty. Since 2007, a similar population shift to urban centers is being led by millennials. Cities in the aggregate have a 0.5 percent growth in jobs annually, so job growth is not the reason. The article says that the reason young people are flocking to cities, with their innovation economies, is the people. Millennials prefer to work with other people in offices, rather than remotely, even though the technology is available. Simply put, they want to be around other smart, creative people.[12]

Access Over Ownership

Millennials are happy to not be shackled to "things." They grew up hearing about the sweatshops that made much of our clothing and the environmental toll of consumerism. Millennials are also happy to find ways to use products that do not involve buying them outright; many companies popping up allow customers to rent or swap items. When I was pregnant, I signed up for the subscription-based clothing rental website Le Tote because I didn't want to pay for maternity clothes I would wear for a few months and then get rid of. If I wanted to keep an item, I simply didn't return the piece from my "tote" and was charged a discounted rate for it.

Venture-backed Le Tote offers both maternity wear and regular women's clothing, and business is booming. When I interviewed the CEO and cofounder, Rakesh Tondon, he said the company's revenue grew 600 percent in 2015. More than 90 percent of the company's customers are repeat purchasers. Le Tote predicted it would send out $400 million worth of product in 2016. Clearly, millennials are interested in engaging with brands in new ways, and companies like Le Tote are taking advantage of these buyers' enthusiasm for fresh customer experiences.

Another venture-backed fashion start-up, Stitch Fix, developed a service that shops for women, matching clients with boutique-brand clothes, shoes, and accessories on recommendations powered by a combination of data science and human stylists. The service offers personalization to a demographic that can't get enough of it. According to *Forbes*,

> customers pay a $20 'styling fee' to receive a box of five personally curated items either on demand or by subscription at regular intervals. They try on the clothes at home, keep what they want and return what they don't. Clients pay the full retail price of any clothes they hold on to, less the $20 fee, which is applied as a credit.[13]

This business model makes perfect sense when you consider how impersonal in-store retail shopping is. When a customer walks into any other store, the store has no clue who she is or what her tastes and preferences are. I mentioned earlier in the book that some retailers are working toward employing facial recognition technology that would send frontline retail employees information about a customer after she walks in the door. But most companies are not there yet.

Every time I go into a large retailer, there appear to be fewer and fewer employees working on the floor to help me find products or answer questions.

While reducing the number of salespeople might save the retailer money in the short term, the tactic will damage the brand in the long term as customers like me eventually switch to options like Stitch Fix, which supply consistent personalized attention. Marka Hansen, former president of Gap North America, sits on Stitch Fix's board and told *Forbes*, "Let's say out of every one hundred customers that come in, twenty-five buy something. Seventy-five had intent to buy, but we don't have any idea why we didn't satisfy them." With personalized clothing services like Le Tote, you simply click the box that matches the reason you didn't like the item. The company can leverage that feedback as it seeks to send you more items to choose from.[14]

Other online fashion start-ups are also changing the game for retail, including ASOS, Nasty Gal, and ModCloth. Some of these brands don't just offer fashion, but they're also becoming trusted advisors to their customers by doing things such as counseling them through the "quarter-life" crisis years. In fact, a few brands riff on this "quarter-life" crisis theme, sympathizing with these twenty-somethings, being a friend when they do or don't feel like "adulting," and empathizing with millennials through other self-deprecating trends they enjoy venting about on social media.[15]

As a company, you have to earn your way into millennials' trusted circles. Increasingly, we're seeing brands revamping their marketing and acting more like confidants of this twenty- to thirty-something crowd facing the trials and tribulations of real life. Brands are partnering with well-loved publishers such as theSkimm, a popular daily newsletter—full of top news—read by your "everywoman," but a newsletter also enjoyed by celebrities like Amy Schumer and Oprah. I've personally been reading this newsletter for a while, and the news bites have some bite to them. They're not serving straight-up news, but rather news with style and a millennial outlook. In addition to money, the company is pulling in advertising in the form of brand sponsorships; it also has a premium app called Skimm Ahead. theSkimm demonstrates that it's no longer enough to provide a product or service—companies must display a cultural understanding. Millennials want companies to know them, listen to them, and show that they understand them.

Millennials demand more from the products and services they consume than customers have at any other time in history. Josh Dykstra of *Fast Company* writes in his article, "Why Millennials Don't Buy Stuff":

Today, a product or service is powerful because of how it connects people to something—or someone—else. It has impact because we can do something worthwhile with it, tell others about it, or have it say something about us.[16]

This is a generation that cares about the environment. They saw their parents' 401K plans and retirement plans disappear overnight. The rampant corruption and environmental damage wrought by companies remains a vivid memory for millennials. Enron, the BP oil spill, and the abuse by major banks has left many millennials mistrusting big business.

Millennials are voting with their wallets, and will pay more for products and services that are built sustainably. According to Nielsen, in 2015, 66 percent of global consumers say they're willing to pay more for sustainable brands—up from 2014.[17] Global environmental issues should be on the agenda of all businesses. Anyone who cares about his or her children's future or even his or her grandchildren's should care about doing business that doesn't destroy the Earth. Consider the words of Craig Wilson, who said in his book *The Compass and the Nail*:

Those who plan for the future of their businesses, in every industry, have to take into the account the increasing scarcity of energy and water and their rising cost, as well as the rising cost of waste and its disposal. Every company—from Walmart to the Cheese Board Collective, from BP to the makers of Fat Tire Ale, from Dow Chemical to Patagonia—is already at work, in some way, even inadvertently, to dismantle a creaky, polluting, wasteful, and increasingly expensive industrial system, and is struggling to create new, less life-draining ways to make things; we are all trying to get a new roof up over the economy before the old, sagging one caves in.

Millennials are cynical about the big businesses that were not environmentally responsible in the last century, and they will pay more for products that were made sustainably—this should be a wake-up call to anyone working at a company focused exclusively on quarterly profits.

Engaging Millennials

Brands need to find innovative ways to engage this demographic that go beyond traditional one-way advertising. If you can't produce creative and catchy content, partner with a well-loved publisher that can help you appeal to a demographic in an inviting way.

I don't watch ads. I find them to be mostly obnoxious interruptions, and I often resent the company interrupting the content I'm viewing, whether it's on TV, YouTube, or publishing platforms. I am positive I have never bought an item after seeing an ad for it, and I have always had problems with the way brands historically represent the customers using their products. Generally, companies don't depict real customers using products in real ways—the word I'm repeating here is *real*. Historically, advertising has suffered from a lack of realness—instead, ads have an element of cheesiness, of fakery, of fantasy. However, we're now seeing more companies attempt to portray real people in their ads and feature genuine stories of their community; advertisers are trying to engage customers in real ways. Millennials need to know you before they'll trust you—are you being real and authentic as you build your relationship with them?[18]

Generation X

Much of what I know about this generation is based on my older brother, Justin, who was born in 1980, the last year that many count as part of generation X. My brother's generation was the first to use computers in college. Being very computer savvy, gen Xers value choice and independence; they tend to be skeptical and self-reliant. That means they do thorough research online before they order products or services. If you want to keep generation X as lifetime customers, consider providing service through a wide range of support channels and allow them plenty of time to ask questions and gather the information they need. They expect the service to be fast and efficient, and would prefer information and choices in real time than wait for a service rep to call them back.[19]

What we can say about generation X is that many of the things that happened when they were coming of age shaped their experiences, similar to the way other world events shaped other generations. During the 1980s, for example, the world was dealing with the AIDS epidemic. There was a lot of fear and misinformation about AIDS at that time—it wasn't until the early 1990s, when celebrities like Magic Johnson started to speak out, that there was greater general awareness about the disease and how it was spread.[20] Generation X was the first generation to enjoy MTV, and some saw their parents fight in the Gulf War (1990–1991).

In a collection of global essays called *Generation X Goes Global: Mapping a Youth Culture in Motion*, Professor Christine Henseler summarizes this group as "a generation whose worldview is based on change, on the need to combat corruption, dictatorships, abuse, AIDS, a generation in search of human dignity and individual freedom, the need for stability, love, tolerance, and human rights for all."[21] In 2007 (before the economic meltdown), a report called "Economic Mobility: Is the American Dream Alive and Well?"[22] claimed that generation X men aged thirty to thirty-nine (those born April 1964 to March 1974) were making 12 percent less than their fathers had at their age. What lifts family income is the fact that many households have two incomes. Women have gone to work, supporting the incomes of men (in heterosexual couples).

Generation X was not without its struggles. But their youth wasn't as war-filled as that of many baby boomers, who we will talk about later, some of whom went overseas to fight in the Vietnam War. Generation X were teenagers that grew up in the cynical grudge rock period of the 1990s, and many held a largely anti-corporate view. Today, this generation has its own children to raise and in the next section, we'll talk about what you can do to engage generation X.[23]

Engaging Gen Xers

This is a generation that does some homework before they contact you. They're also juggling a lot of home stresses, so generation X will love you if your self-service is clean and easy to use. Websites should not only flow easily, they should be fast. Because members of generation X often have little in savings, they are not going to be charmed if you attempt to charge them for every service repair for the product. They are a no-nonsense generation of straight shooters. Don't try to pull any fast ones on this serious and sometimes cynical generation.[24]

Baby Boomers

I'm always impressed by the technical savvy of baby boomers. While some baby boomers—born between 1946 and 1964—like Steve Jobs and Steve Wozniak—were building computers in the 1980s, not all baby boomers embraced tech to such a degree. Even so, baby boomers are often the biggest users of technology. Perhaps because they enjoy using Skype and Facebook to engage with their grandchildren, they are often super users of social technologies. Today, baby boomers reminisce about a life without instant gratification, Snapchat, and Starbucks. As a group, they are the wealthiest, most activist generation.

Baby boomers are probably the last generation that will receive a pension, though many of those on the younger end of the spectrum will not. Many received their peak levels of income during a time period when it wasn't hard to buy a house. This generation was supposedly the first to be, from birth, dissected, analyzed, and pitched to by marketers. It takes time to accrue money, and this generation has time on their side. They control 80 percent of personal financial assets and more than half of all consumer spending. They purchase 77 percent of all prescription drugs, 61 percent of over-the-counter drugs, and 80 percent of all leisure travel.[25]

According to "Crafting the Customer Experience for People Not Like You: How to Delight and Engage the Customers Your Competitors Don't Understand" by Kelly McDonald, boomers are independent thinkers who pride themselves on being nonconforming individuals.

Engaging Baby Boomers

This generation doesn't want to be bothered with trickery or handled with overly aggressive sales and marketing tactics. They are described as being demanding and inquisitive consumers. Attributes that reflect a boomer-friendly customer experience are integrity and courtesy. Provide the facts and avoid overselling this generation, and you will earn their trust.[26] They see themselves as adventurous, open-minded, and progressive, and they like to be known for these things. They do not want to be made to feel vulnerable, and they pride themselves on being highly informed. According to McDonald, you need to remove risk to provide a great customer experience for boomers. For baby boomers, the ideal customer experience is one that they get to create. They seek experiences where they get all the information about the opportunity but then have the freedom to explore on their own, unlike their parents (known as the matures), who like to have things scheduled; this tendency has bearing for the travel industry more than any other.

This generation is also concerned with the rights of the consumer. When you create your return policy, communicate that you have taken everyone's rights and best interests into consideration as you address problems.[27]

***

You will always benefit from knowing your customers. Having a better understanding of larger cultural factors, and the trends that shape generations, will only help you make better decisions for your customers. And, though strong research is important, don't forget to talk to your customers and actually ask them what they like.

Notes

1. Corey Seemiller and Meghan Grace, *Generation Z Goes to College*, 1st ed. (San Francisco: Jossey-Bass, 2016).
2. Jim Edwards, "Goldman Sachs Has a Chart of the Generations and It Will Make the Generations Shudder," *Business Insider*, December 5, 2015, www.businessinsider.com/goldman-sachs-chart-of-the-generations-and-gen-z-2015–12.
3. Amanda Lenhart, "Cell Phone Ownership," *Pew Research Center*, March 19, 2012, www.pewinternet.org/2012/03/19/cell-phone-ownership/.
4. Matt Kleinschmit, "Generation Z Characteristics: 5 Infographics on the Gen Z Lifestyle," *Vision Critical Communications*, December 4, 2015, www.visioncritical.com/generation-z-infographics.
5. Jasmine Paul, "Marketing to Millennials? Meh. The Future Is Gen Z," *Mad Fish Digital*, July 20, 2016, www.madfishdigital.com/blog/genz-marketing-millennials/.
6. The Upfront Analytics Team, "Marketing to Generation Z Teenagers: 10 Awesome Tips," *The Upfront Analytics*, November 4, 2015, http://upfrontanalytics.com/marketing-generation-z-infographic/.
7. Aaron Paquette, "Ad Blocking and Teen Engagement: Here's What Marketers Need to Know," *MediaPost Communications*, October 8, 2015, www.mediapost.com/publications/article/260049/ad-blocking-and-teen-engagement-heres-what-marke.html.
8. Alison Syrett, "How Millennials Labels Are Bringing Brand Loyalty Back," *Fashionista*, June 14, 2016, http://fashionista.com/2016/06/brand-loyalty-millennials.
9. "Millennials: Fueling the Experience Economy," *Eventbrite*, November 20, 2016, http://eventbrite-s3.s3.amazonaws.com/marketing/Millennials_Research/Gen_PR_Final.pdf.
10. Tamar Frumkin, "5 Ways Millennials Are Re-Defining the Customer Experience," *Sales Force*, April 9, 2015, www.salesforce.com/blog/2015/04/5-ways-millennials-re-defining-customer-experience-gp.html.
11. Richard Fry, "For First Time in Modern Era, Living with Parents Edges out Other Living Arrangements for 18- to 34-Year-Olds," *Pew Research Center*, May 24, 2016, www.pewsocialtrends.org/2016/05/24/for-first-time-in-modern-era-living-with-parents-edges-out-other-living-arrangements-for-18-to-34-year-olds/.
12. Kevin Maney, "Why Millennials Still Move to Cites," *Newsweek*, March 30, 2015, www.newsweek.com/2015/04/10/why-cities-hold-more-pull-millennials-cloud-317735.html.

13. Ryan Mac, "Stitch Fix: The $250 Million Startup Playing Fashionista Money-ball," *Forbes*, June 1, 2016, www.forbes.com/sites/ryanmac/2016/06/01/fashionista-moneyball-stitch-fix-katrina-lake/#549c2a662e2e.

14. Ibidem.

15. Tanya Dua, "Brands Are Counseling the Young and the Traumatized through Their #Quarterlifecrisis," *Digiday*, 2016, http://digiday.com/brands/brands-counseling-millennials-quarterlife-crises/.

16. Josh Allan Dykstra, "Why Millennials Don't Want to Buy Stuff," *Fast Company*, July 13, 2012, www.fastcompany.com/1842581/why-millennials-dont-want-buy-stuff.

17. Andrew McCaskill, "Consumer-Goods' Brands That Demonstrate Commitment to Sustainability Outperform Those That Don't," *Nielsen.Com*, October 12, 2015, www.nielsen.com/us/en/press-room/2015/consumer-goods-brands-that-demonstrate-commitment-to-sustainability-outperform.html.

18. Matthew Tyson, "Millennials Want Brands to Be More Authentic: Here's Why That Matters," *The Huffington Post*, January 21, 2016, www.huffingtonpost.com/matthew-tyson/millennials-want-brands-t_b_9032718.html.

19. Julia Lewis, "How to Deliver Exceptional Service to Four Generations of Customers," *Provide Support*, April 16, 2015, www.providesupport.com/blog/four-generations-of-customers.

20. Phillip Zonkel, "AIDS Crisis Loomed over Generation X," *Long Beach Press Telegram*, February 1, 2016, www.presstelegram.com/health/20160102/aids-crisis-loomed-over-generation-x.

21. "Generation X," *Generational Research Foundation*, November 21, 2016, www.generationalresearchfoundation.com/generation-x.

22. The Pew Charitable Trusts, *Economic Mobility: Is the American Dream Alive and Well?* 1st ed. (Philadelphia: The Pew Charitable Trusts, 2007).

23. *Wikipedia*, s.v. "Generation X," last modified November 17, 2016, https://en.wikipedia.org/wiki/Generation_X#cite_note-Isabel_Sawhill.2C_Ph.D_2007-47.

24. Chris Bennington, "How Different Generations Prefer Different Customer Service," *Cincom Systems*, November 27, 2012, www.cincom.com/blog/customer-communications/how-different-generations-prefer-different-customer-service/.

25. *Wikipedia*, s.v. "Baby Boomers," last modified November 19, 2016, https://en.wikipedia.org/wiki/Baby_boomers.

26. Benington, "How Different Generations Prefer Different Customer Service."

27. Kelly McDonald, *Crafting the Customer Experience for People Not Like You: How to Delight and Engage the Customers Your Competitors Don't Understand* (Hoboken, NJ: Wiley & Sons, 2013).

CHAPTER 14

Making It Right With Your Customers

Matthew Dixon and Nick Toman, authors of *The Effortless Experience*, penned an article with Karen Freeman in the *Harvard Business Review* called "Stop Trying to Delight Your Customers." They wrote about a research study done by the Customer Contact Council, a division of the Corporate Executive Board, that was conducted with 75,000 people who had interacted over the phone with contact center representatives or through self-service channels such as the web, voice prompts, chat, or e-mail. Delighting customers, they found, doesn't build loyalty, but add "reducing their [the customers'] effort—the work they must do to get their problem solved—does."

Essentially, the authors argue that focusing on customer delight is a waste of time—don't go above and beyond. While I agree that reducing customer effort and running a more efficient operation increases customer satisfaction and loyalty, I believe running a culture of customer delight impacts the internal culture of the company. In contrast to a culture of delight, how do employees feel when they must tell customers no all day? They are told to stick to scripts and they cannot offer extras for problems that occur. This is how most contact centers are run, with employees kept on short leashes. The entire operation runs strictly in order to spend as little money as possible.

Most companies believe the contact center has nothing to do with relationship building, but when agents feel like they have authority to do things that sincerely delight customers, the contact center culture is affected in powerful and positive ways. If you raise the level of the culture, granting agents room and budgets to do things for customers, you clearly change the way the agents feel, and that changes the way customers feel.

Is this really the time to rain down on the companies that focus on customer delight? While, as the article says, delighting customers is a "Herculean effort," it's still a noble and important pursuit. Most companies provide abysmal customer experiences, and it can be hard to tell who is more miserable, customers or employees. But when customers are miserable, employees are miserable too. And when employees are miserable, customers are likewise miserable.

Next, let's talk about how and why customer delight is generally a good idea.

Case Study: Hilton Worldwide's Make It Right Program

Mark Weinstein, SVP and global head of customer engagement, loyalty, and partnerships for Hilton Worldwide, who defined customer experience earlier in the book, believes in delighting customers, but he adds that when you build an infrastructure to enable the culture, it's no longer "customer delight": it's simply how your company operates. Weinstein spoke with me about Hilton Worldwide's "delight" program—he recognizes that, at times, delight programs can be degrading. In essence, "You've boiled down my day of inconvenience for a few cents." Let's say a customer's flight is delayed and she misses an important event like a wedding. The delay was the airline's fault. For service recovery, that customer is then given a few bonus miles for the inconvenience. That's almost worse than if the company did nothing. Not doing enough in service recovery can backfire on the company.

Adding up the cost of all the moments, Weinstein says, doesn't create a strong impact for the customer. For example, you're at a movie and the movie freezes. The movie theater calculates that, for your inconvenience, the theater will enter you in a contest to win a soda. This offer trivializes the customer experience. When Hilton Worldwide decided it wanted to do something different with its service recovery program, there was an internal debate about what proper service recovery looks like. Eventually, Hilton rolled out a program to all its brands called the "Make It Right" program. If there's a customer problem, the agent is empowered to refund the full amount of the hotel stay to the customer. After rolling out this program, Hilton realized it cost the same to refund the full amount that it would to provide a freebie here or there.

Hilton Worldwide believes in empowering its agents to achieve first-call resolution—the company doesn't want customers calling ten times, and customers don't want that either! With every call, the company is doing its best to route the customer to the person who can solve the problem. There are limits and penalties, though—it's not a free for all. While there are extreme examples, such as during storms, where Hilton is refunding mass numbers of customers for inconveniences, the company sets those aside and looks at averages and service recovery across its hotels. Hilton headquarters—if it sees repeat offenders, such as a property with a lot of refunds going out—charges repeat offenders an administrative fee, in order to encourage those hotels to review the underlying problem and address root issues. Headquarters wants the individual properties to have skin in the game. "We have a partnership among the hotel, the teams, and the brand to deliver a customer experience," said Weinstein.

Case Study: Online Retailer Zulily Acts Human

A culture that delights is one that accounts for customer variation. Agents aren't forced to use scripts! As consumers, most of us can think of a time when we had an emergency, and a brand either left an imprint on our memory by going out of its way to help us or the brand told us no and left us with a very bad taste in our mouth. Ideally, agents will meet customers where the customers feel comfortable engaging with us, and we will go outside of normal processes when it makes sense. Consider this story, which features online flash deals site Zulily; it recounts a woman's experience with her purchase. The woman is Kelly Blue Kinkel, and in a public Facebook post in 2016, she wrote:

> I sincerely hope this post goes viral, because I just hung up from one
> of the best customer service experiences of my life. I ordered a winter

coat from Zulily a few weeks ago. When I received my order, I could see through the packaging that the coat material wasn't going to work well with the two breeds of dogs we have. Coarse dog hair and certain materials don't mix. I called customer service and asked how to return the unopened coat for a refund. I spoke with a sweet young man named Patrick, and he let me know he would refund my money immediately. I asked again how to send it back, and he said, "Please don't send it back. If you know someone who needs a winter coat or if you would like to donate it to a charity, that would make us very happy." I honestly thought he was kidding. It took me a moment to realize he was completely serious, and then came the tears. I just don't know other companies that do this, do you? I thought Zulily was pretty incredible before, but after today, I'm a customer for LIFE. The world needs more LOVE like that. Honest business. Honest ethics. How refreshing!

This post generated 134,000 views and 60,000 shares. It always pays to do the right thing—but doing the right thing demands a culture in which employees can make judgment calls, one in which they are operating without having a script. Not only did this story generate a ton of attention for Zulily, but I'm sure it referred business their way as well.[1]

The business environment today demands that we make accommodations for customers. We must allow employees to do right by the customer, even if it means going outside standard processes.

Delighting Customers Saves Time!

Let's talk about time. When you empower your agents to get things done without approval, you save your company a lot of time. Consider this quote from George Stalk, author of the 1989 *Competing Against Time: How Time-Based Competition Is Reshaping Global Markets*:

Capitalizing on time [is] a critical source of competitive advantage: shortening the planning loop in the product development cycle, trimming process time in the factory, drastically reducing sales and distribution—managing time the way most companies manage costs, quality, or inventory. In fact, as a strategic weapon, time is the equivalent of money, productivity, quality, even innovation.[2]

The Customer Experience Performance Gap

There is no more evolved customer experience than that offered by Amazon. It completely threw out the rules for what a transaction looked like and wrote its own bible.

Amazon Prime, originally called "Free Super Saver Shipping Offer," launched in 2000. Applicable only for items over $100, it proved to be powerful word-of-mouth marketing, and set the benchmark for the entire industry. With Amazon Prime, two-day delivery is standard, and more than a million items on the site (as of June 2016) can be delivered the same day. In fact, a new study conducted by Deutsche Bank shows that customers double the amount they spend on Amazon after becoming a member of the Amazon Prime subscription service.[3] The bank surveyed twenty Amazon Prime customers who, together, had made more than 5,000 orders in over a decade. The survey found that spending increased 100 percent after a customer signed up for Prime.

Customers will pay more for better service, and when they receive better service, they also buy more. Amazon has an estimated 69 million Amazon Prime members, and in fact, Amazon Prime members now outnumber regular Amazon customers.[4] Amazon provides the most seamless shopping and return experience available today;[5] with a few clicks, you can easily return an item. Now, with Amazon returns, the company will also pick items up—you don't have to drive anywhere at all.

Jeff Bezos, Amazon's CEO, has talked about starting with customer needs, about innovating by working backward from customer needs. Bezos knew customers wanted better prices and products delivered to them faster and more conveniently, and he has led Amazon to build a compelling customer journey. But the vast and efficient marketplace Amazon has built is not its only contribution—Amazon is innovating the way people buy. It has connected its Amazon virtual assistant, the Echo, with the customer's shopping cart. A customer can talk to the Echo's virtual assistant, named Alexa, asking questions and ordering products: Do you want to know how many grams in a kilo? Ask Alexa. Want to play your Spotify list? Alexa will happily help you. Additionally, the Amazon Echo can control smart devices by functioning as a home automation hub.

Amazon Echo is one of the most efficient voice command devices out there. In the future, we will be talking not just to Siri and Alexa but to many of our products. Amazon, with its commitment to fulfilling customer needs and providing a seamless shopping experience, has grown quickly. In 2015, 51 percent of U.S. consumers planned to do holiday shopping on Amazon. com. Considering the size of the web, this is no small feat.[6]

Jeff Bezos once said, "In the old world, you devoted thirty percent of your time to building a great service and seventy percent of your time to shouting about it. In the new world, that inverts."[7]

Great companies start with customer need. For these companies, building an excellent product for their customers takes most of their time, rather than spending most of their time marketing the product and broadcasting about it. Bezos also reportedly said,

> When [competitors are] in the shower in the morning, they're thinking about how they're going to get ahead of one of their top competitors. Here in the shower, we're thinking about how we are going to invent something on behalf of a customer.[8]

It's that customer obsession that separates great companies from good companies. Today's best products are about utility—they need to serve a purpose, or else they will be swallowed up by the competition. Are your products and services making customers' lives easier?

But even a company as great as Amazon is not perfect. In fact, today I called Amazon to find out if it would price match a beautiful patio set I had found on Wayfair, a competitive website. I reached an agent who transferred me to another agent. I asked him where he was based, curious to know where Amazon kept its call centers; he told me Jamaica. The agent asked me to add the item in question to my cart, which I did. He put me on hold and came back muttering something about being sorry he would be missing out on something later. He then realized he forgot to mute me and was embarrassed about what he'd said. I asked him what he was missing out on and he told me some chips that were being shared. I told him he should grab some so as not to miss out. After all, I was in a good mood since I thought this department was taking my inquiry seriously about this expensive patio set I wanted price matched.

Then, after about fifteen minutes, I was forwarded to a third agent, who apologized because Amazon no longer does price matching for anything but televisions. She said she was sorry, but there was nothing she could do. Since I've never talked to anyone in the Amazon call center, I was disappointed that the agent did not communicate this policy at the beginning of my call. Even at Amazon, customers can be thrown around like a hot potato and, at the end, the customer makes no progress, which hurts the relationship. No company is perfect, and most companies are far from perfect in shaping their customer experiences—it's a matter of how far.

Consider the graphic, the "Customer Experience Performance Gap," which I built to show the differences between companies that offer incredible experiences and those that offer poor ones. The customer must be the focal point of the company, with products and services iterated obsessively until they meet the majority of customer needs. A customer culture generally boasts a stronger employee culture overall. After ensuring culture, vision and values are ingrained in the company—technology is paramount. The brand can't move forward without the right technology. This technology will allow the company to create a unified workflow. The company shouldn't have separate tools for separate channels. The employee experience needs to be just as seamless and easy as the customer experience.

Certain strategies and technologies have to be in place if the brand is to successfully meet customers on the channels those customers are already using. The more channels the brand tries to support—without the proper mechanism—the worse the customer experience. The more the company is equipped to handle an increasing number of channels, the bigger the positive impact on customer service—and customer experience. But proper technology and strategies need to be in place for that to happen.

Dissecting the Customer Experience Performance Gap

In the "Customer Experience Performance Gap," the bottom right bubble, labeled 5, is the company that needs the most work when it comes to its customer experience. This low performer would greatly benefit from having a customer relationship management tool (CRM). It would also be more

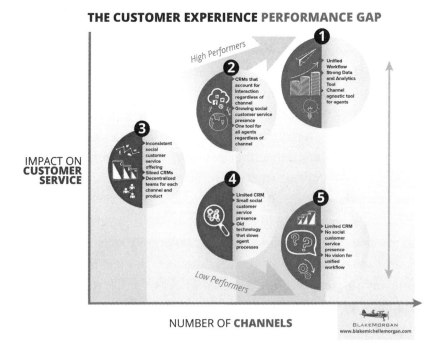

Figure 14.1 *The Customer Experience Performance Gap*

successful if it offered social customer service on Twitter or Facebook. This laggard lacks what I talked about earlier in the book, a vision for a unified workflow. This company is in no position to prepare for the increasing number of channels customers seek to engage on. This company is absolutely not competing on customer experience.

A little better than the lowest performer, company 4 has a small-scale CRM and a tiny social media customer service offering. The company has one person attempting to manage Twitter and Facebook, but this employee checks the accounts only a few times a day in the company's own time zone. The old technology is layered and layered, creating a very long and slow process for the customer service agent. The customer experience is not appealing, and this company is in no position to help customers on more than a few traditional channels.

Company 3 shows some progress, but is still not doing enough. The company has a social customer service offering, although it's limited. This company will answer your tweet but will redirect you to a call center (providing the phone number to that center). The description for company 3 describes organizations such as banks that send you e-mail with forms you must print out and fax to them. Who wants to fax? Company 3 has many different technologies within the company—various departments use separate CRMs, for example. Often, these technologies are sold by completely different vendors, which makes it impossible customer data to be shared—a complete headache for employees who are trying to provide customer service. There is no central tool, and as a result, customers who contact various departments have various experiences.

Company 2 is much better. This company has a CRM with some real power, accounting for interactions regardless of channel. That means the CRM can accommodate all channels, such as text, e-mail, phone, Weibo, WeChat, video customer service, Twitter, Snapchat, Facebook Messenger, and more. This company has a powerful social customer service presence, and it's evolving to serve customers on an increasing number of channels. This is a company that meets the customer where the customer is, and the technology makes it easy for agents to do that. The agents enjoy a unified workflow, and they share information and collaborate around one easy-to-use piece of technology. This company is on the road to best-in-class customer experience.

Company 1 features a unified workflow—the agent isn't working in and out of ten disparate systems. Instead, the agent uses one tool for a variety of channels. This tool features powerful data and analytics components, creating a robust customer experience. For example, when the agent interacts with the customer, the agent knows specific, real-time customer data about the customer's location, what she's experiencing, and what would be most helpful to her in at that moment. The customer never has to repeat herself.

Consider the innovation coming out of the Internet of Things (IoT). If the company were to tap into the Internet of Things, the agent could get real-time updates sent to him with key insights into the customer's current location. With IoT, the customer's product will communicate directly with the company, without the customer having to initiate. Company 1 on this infograph shows that it has provided agents with tools that offer extreme flexibility. An agent can be working in Twitter, Facebook, Snapchat, a chat technology, or even on the phone, and the CRM will accommodate that agent wherever he is.

***

In this chapter, we looked at how some of the best companies are working to make things right with their customers when service goes awry or products fail. We talked about Hilton's "make it right" program and how the online retailer Zulily acts human. We reviewed how delighting customers saves your brand time, and closed by discussing the customer experience performance gap. While you don't need to mimic these companies in everything they do, broadening your thinking about the way your company approaches customer strategy sets you up to create compelling customer experiences. In the next chapter, we'll talk about how your outlook on profits shapes the way you do business.

Notes

1. Kim LaCapria, "Zulily Rejects Winter Coat Return, Suggests Donating It to the Needy," *Urban Legends Reference Pages*, January 13, 2016, www.snopes.com/2016/01/13/zulily-rejects-winter-coat/#.
2. Steve Denning, "Is Delighting the Customer Profitable?" *Forbes*, April 1, 2011, www.forbes.com/sites/stevedenning/2011/04/01/is-delighting-the-customer-profitable/#af9cd6a151bd.
3. John Rossman, *The Amazon Way: 14 Leadership Principles behind the World's Most Disruptive Company* (CreateSpace Independent Publishing Platform, 2014).
4. Audrey Shi, "Amazon Prime Members Now Outnumber Non-Prime Customers," *Fortune*, July 11, 2016, http://fortune.com/2016/07/11/amazon-prime-customers/.
5. James Cook, "Here's How Much Amazon Prime Customers Spend Every Year after They Become Members," *Business Insider*, June 15, 2016, www.businessinsider.com/how-much-amazon-prime-customers-spend-every-year-after-they-become-members-2016–6?platform=hootsuite.
6. Matt Rosoff, "More Than Half of Americans Will Do 'Most' of Their Holiday Shopping at Amazon," *Business Insider*, December 17, 2015, www.businessinsider.com/amazon-dominates-holiday-shopping-2015–12?utm_source=feedly&utm_medium=webfeeds.
7. Morgan Housel, "The 20 Smartest Things Jeff Bezos Has Ever Said," *The Motley Fool*, September 9, 2013, www.fool.com/investing/general/2013/09/09/the-25-smartest-things-jeff-bezos-has-ever-said.aspx.
8. Adam Lashinsky, "Amazon's Jeff Bezos: The Ultimate Disrupter," *Fortune*, November 16, 2012, http://fortune.com/2012/11/16/amazons-jeff-bezos-the-ultimate-disrupter/.

CHAPTER 15

A Focus on Quarterly Profits Kills Long-Term Growth

Most CEOs focus solely on short-term profits, a habit satirized on the well-loved HBO television series *Silicon Valley*. The show follows the story of an innovative start-up called Pied Piper. A new CEO (Jack) is hired to replace the founder (Richard) as CEO, and with the change comes new attitudes and approaches. In a discussion about what the product they're selling actually is, Jack tells Richard, "The product isn't the platform, and the product isn't your algorithm either, and it's not even the software. Do you know what Pied Piper's product is?" "Is it me?" Richard asks, as inspirational music builds behind him. "Oh, God! No! No!" Jack shrieks. "Pied Piper's product is its stock. Whatever makes the value of that stock go up, that is what we're going to make."[1] In an interview with Terri Gross, host of NPR's *Fresh Air*, show creators Mike Judge and Alec Berg talk about the irony of *Silicon Valley* itself, where Bay Area hippie culture meets the cut-throat tech scene. There comes a point in every company's growth where compromises are made in pursuit of financial growth.

But some real-life CEOs are taking stances against the pressures of Wall Street. In a *Bloomberg* video interview, JPMorgan Chase & Co. CEO Jamie Dimon said, "Corporate leaders shouldn't give earnings guidance because they can't predict the future and should focus instead on long-term performance."[2] Dimon said some CEOs "start making promises they shouldn't make." He warns others, "Don't make earnings forecasts. You don't know what's going to happen every quarter. I don't even care about quarterly earnings."[3] Can you imagine if every company thought that way?

Amazon.com doesn't focus on quarterly profits but instead on long-term gains. CEO and founder Jeff Bezos isn't handcuffed to the pressure of quarterly profits because he owns 20 percent of Amazon, more than 87 million shares. Amazon is able to take more risks and give them time to gel because Bezos, the guy steering the ship, doesn't feel beholden to investors the way many other CEOs do.[4]

Consider professor and author Roger Martin's comments in "The Age of Customer Capitalism,"[5] in which he shows how a focus on maximizing profitability tends to lead companies to undermine long-term profitability. He writes, "The harder a CEO is pushed to increase shareholder value, the more the CEO will be tempted to make moves that actually hurt the shareholders." In the article, he cites as an example Jack Welch, famous for transforming GE from a firm with a market capitalization of $13 billion in 1981 into the world's most valuable company, worth $484 billion by 2001. Welch pushed and pushed GE to achieve more growth, and he used GE Capital to do so (GE Capital is a financial services firm that provides commercial lending and leasing, in addition to other services). However, in 2009, after GE took large write-offs related to GE Capital, GE's market capitalization fell to $75 billion.[6]

Martin wrote:

While the $471 billion increase in shareholder value that Welch over-saw seemed wonderful at the time of his retirement, particularly to shareholders selling out at the top, it is questionable how much share-holders benefited in the long term." Welch, once the poster boy for shareholder value, later admitted to the *Financial Times*, "Shareholder value is the dumbest idea in the world. Shareholder value is a result, not a strategy . . . your main constituencies are your employees, your customers and your products.[7]

What Are Bad Profits?

Author and speaker Steve Denning writes about "bad profits" in a *Forbes* article titled "Is Delighting the Customer Profitable?" Bad profits are those that come from acting in unscrupulous ways. Denning quotes author Fred

Reichheld's *The Ultimate Question* (2006):[8] "Whenever a customer feels misled, mistreated, ignored or coerced, then profits from that customer are bad." According to Reichheld, companies generate bad profits when they deliver a poor customer experience. Bad profits come from extracting value from customers, pushing overpriced products on trusting customers, duping customers with confusing pricing schemes, and related shady activities.[9]

Marketing, sales, product development, engineering, HR, and finance all have a hand in the kinds of profits a company generates. While technology has made many aspects of our lives easier at work and at home, there are still no shortcuts. If something seems too good to be true, it is. Building incredible products and services takes obsessive attention to detail. It takes hard work and a considerable amount of time spent thinking about the person you are creating the product or service for. If you personally wouldn't use the product or service you're selling, or wouldn't sell the product to your close friends or family, it's a significant wake-up call that you're operating in a bad business.

These bad profits will eventually destroy your business. It's not worth it! The only way to run a business is to look at the horizon, think about tomorrow, and consider the repercussions of all the decisions you make. It is very important to your efforts to build relationships with customers based on mutual respect; this type of relationship means not seeing every customer with a dollar sign on her head. To think long term, executives need to run their business as if they are in the relationship business.

We Appreciate Your Patience

If there's anything that will make you feel like a number on a spreadsheet, it's air travel. Today's airlines are still trying to do more with less, stuffing an increasing number of customers into a smaller amount of space. And have you noticed it takes longer to get through airport security? In 2016, we learned that the governing body that runs TSA spent the money it was supposed to use to improve efficiencies on non-TSA things. In that same year, the U.S. Congress and the White House diverted $12.6 billion in passenger security fees to reduce the deficit over the next decade in a classic case of bait-and-switch taxation.

When you are on a flight and you're sitting on the tarmac for an extended period of time, the pilot will often make an announcement. If the pilot is delivering bad news, he will often say, "We want to thank you for your patience." Most customers listening will think to themselves, "Patience? No one asked me if I was being patient! I'm mad as hell!" Clearly, customers have no choice in the matter. They are stuck in a seat on a locked plane. The pilot is communicating to customers, "We are taking your time, and thank you for letting us do that." This is not a two-way communication, in which customers tell the staff, "Don't worry about it, we'll gladly be patient for you." This is the staff broadcasting a one-way communication.

A "thank you for your patience" message is worse than an apology because it makes assumptions about what the customers are going through. This is one of the millions of examples of the way companies take time away from customers and don't have an empathetic attitude when they do so. The brand is in control, the customer isn't. As I sat on a flight where we waited and waited and waited for a gate to open so our flight could unload, I wondered what the airline industry would be like if Jeff Bezos took over. I couldn't help but imagine a more efficient, elegant, and easy experience.

***

What's your business's version of the message on the airplane's radio to customers? Most companies have some form of "thank you for your patience." It's time to do away with these customer repellants. When it comes to revamping your customer experience, the best way to do it is to do it. Start today. Just because you've always run your business one way doesn't mean you can't change starting today. Be the company that decides to focus on long-term growth rather than short-term profits.

Notes

1. David Sims, "Silicon Valley's Sad Ballad of Start-Up Success," *The Atlantic Monthly Group*, May 2, 2016, www.theatlantic.com/entertainment/archive/2016/05/silicon-valleys-sad-ballad-of-tech-success/480849/.

2. Dimon, Jamie, "Jamie Dimon To CEO's: Don't Make Earnings Forecasts," *Bloomberg Video*, October 12, 2015, www.bloomberg.com/news/videos/2015–10–19/jamie-dimon-to-ceos-don-t-make-earnings-forecasts-.

3. Hugh Son and Claire Boston, "Dimon Says CEOs Should Focus More on Long Term, Not Analysts," *Bloomberg*, October 19, 2015, www.bloomberg.com/news/articles/2015–10–19/dimon-says-ceos-should-abstain-from-giving-guidance-on-earnings.

4. John Rossman, *The Amazon Way: 14 Leadership Principles behind the World's Most Disruptive Company* (CreateSpace Independent Publishing Platform, 2014).

5. Roger Martin, "The Age of Customer Capitalism," *Harvard Business Review*, January–February 2010 Issue, https://hbr.org/2010/01/the-age-of-customer-capitalism.

6. Steve Denning, "Is Delighting the Customer Profitable?" *Forbes*, April 1, 2011, www.forbes.com/sites/stevedenning/2011/04/01/is-delighting-the-customer-profitable/#ac16cc7151bd.

7. Steve Denning, "The Origin of 'The World's Dumbest Idea': Milton Friedman," *Forbes*, June 26, 2013, www.forbes.com/sites/stevedenning/2013/06/26/the-origin-of-the-worlds-dumbest-idea-milton-friedman/#2683daed214c.

8. Denning, "Is Delighting the Customer Profitable?"

9. Ibidem.

Conclusion

When I ask the most successful leaders and employees why they like working with customers, they always tell me they like being there at the point of need. When employees' work is meaningful, it becomes more enjoyable. When they can see the direct benefits of their work, they become inspired to give more. The entire concept behind D.O.M.O.R.E. is that coasting by on the success you've had in the past is no longer enough. You must work hard every single day, as if you're at square one.

This is an exciting time to be talking about customer experience. We've never had greater potential to design compelling customer experiences than we have today. The digital landscape is not for the faint of heart, but if you can hire customer experience leaders who have the ability to distill a complicated customer landscape into a simple strategy, you will be thankful for hiring that individual. Today's brands need a vision for tomorrow: no matter where you are on your customer experience journey, now is the time to be thoughtful and deliberate about customer experience. The entire industry is on the brink of an innovation explosion. All the stars are aligned as key executives become more aware of the importance of building authentic customer relationships. Most marketers today are aware of the importance of having a customer strategy, and most CEOs understand the importance of organizing the company around the customer rather than vice versa.

Technology is a prime reason we are on the brink of so much exciting change for the industry. Many of the technologies I've talked about in this book, including artificial intelligence, the Internet of Things, robots, CRM, data, personalization, and omnichannel tools, will make life better for both customers and the companies that seek to engage them. I've talked extensively about content and the critical role it plays in your customer experience offering. That means you need to hire people who are brilliant communicators. You will benefit from hiring a diverse team—creative writers in addition to brilliant engineers—who understand the customer's journey.

More Is More has shown you what may seem obvious but that too many miss. Have you ever lost your sunglasses and found that they were on your head the entire time? Sometimes the answer you've been searching for is right in front of your face, but you are so bogged down with day-to-day matters that you can't see it. Be the company that doesn't miss the obvious. You are now equipped to start making change at your company. You have everything you need to begin improving your customer experience today. The future is just on the horizon. The technology in the personal lives of your customers has only increased their expectations for the ways in which your brand will interact with them. You have a huge opportunity ahead of you—all it takes is a change in thinking about your customers and the role they play in your business.

References

Adamczyk, Alicia. "Sears, Walmart, Target & Others That Have or Will Close Stores in 2016." *Time*, April 22, 2016. http://time.com/money/4304622/stores-closing-in-2016/.

Anthony, Scott. "What Do You Really Mean by Business 'Transformation'?" *Harvard Business Review*, February 29, 2016. https://hbr.org/2016/02/what-do-you-really-mean-by-business-transformation.

Baer, Jay. *Hug Your Haters: How to Embrace Complaints and Keep Your Customers*. London: Penguin/Portfolio, 2013.

Bennington, Chris. "How Different Generations Prefer Different Customer Service." *Cincom Systems*, November 27, 2012. www.cincom.com/blog/customer-communications/how-different-generations-prefer-different-customer-service/.

Berger, Warren. "Why Curious People Are Destined for the C-Suite." *Harvard Business Review*, September 11, 2015. https://hbr.org/2015/09/why-curious-people-are-destined-for-the-c-suite.

Bharat. "How Much Data Do We Generate Every Day." *Digital Callout*, November 21, 2015. www.digitalcallout.com/2015/12/how-much-data-do-we-generate-every-day.html?m=1.

Bliss, Jeanne. 2006. *Chief Customer Officer: Getting Past Lip Service to Passionate Action*. New York: Wiley/Jossey-Bass.

Brehm, Kayla. "7 Facts That Show That Customer Service Is More Profitable Than Sales." *Help.com*, September 22, 2014. https://blog.help.com/2014/09/22/7-facts-that-show-that-customer-service-is-more-profitable-than-sales/.

Brown, David, Veronica Melian, Marc Solow, Sonny Chheng, and Kathy Parker. "Culture and Engagement: The Naked Organization." *Deloitte University Press*,

February 27, 2015. https://dupress.deloitte.com/dup-us-en/focus/human-capital-trends/2015/employee-engagement-culture-human-capital-trends-2015.html.

Conlin, Michelle. "Netflix: Recruiting and Retaining the Best Talent." *Bloomberg*, September 14, 2007. www.bloomberg.com/news/articles/2007–09–13/netflix-recruiting-and-retaining-the-best-talentbusinessweek-business-news-stock-market-and-financial-advice.

Cook, James. "Here's How Much Amazon Prime Customers Spend Every Year after They Become Members." *Business Insider*, June 15, 2016. www.businessinsider.com/how-much-amazon-prime-customers-spend-every-year-after-they-become-members-2016–6?platform=hootsuite.

Cook, Tony, Tom LoBianco, and Doug Stanglin. "Indiana Governor Signs Amended 'Religious Freedom' Law." *USA Today*, April 2, 2015. www.usatoday.com/story/news/nation/2015/04/02/indiana-religious-freedom-law-deal-gay-discrimination/70819106/.

Denning, Steve. "Is Delighting the Customer Profitable?" *Forbes*, April 1, 2011. www.forbes.com/sites/stevedenning/2011/04/01/is-delighting-the-customer-profitable/#ac16cc7151bd.

Denning, Steve. "The Origin of 'The World's Dumbest Idea': Milton Friedman." *Forbes*, June 26, 2013. www.forbes.com/sites/stevedenning/2013/06/26/the-origin-of-the-worlds-dumbest-idea-milton-friedman/#2683daed214c.

Discovery. "Discovery Channel's 2010–11 Upfront Slate Is Filled with Epic Specials, Favorite Long-Run Series and Exciting New Talent." April 8, 2010. https://corporate.discovery.com/discovery-newsroom/discovery-channels-2010–11-upfront-slate-is-filled/.

Dixon, Matthew, Karen Freeman, and Nicholas Toman. "Stop Trying to Delight Your Customers." *Harvard Business Review*, July–August 2010. https://hbr.org/2016/02/what-do-you-really-mean-by-business-transformation.

Dixon, Matthew, Nick Toman, and Rick Delisi. *The Effortless Experience: Conquering the New Battleground for Customer Loyalty*. London: Penguin/Portfolio, 2013.

Docherty, Michael. *Collective Disruption*. 1st ed. Boca Raton, FL: Polarity Press, 2015.

Dockterman, Eliana. "Uber and Lyft Are Leaving Austin after Losing Background Check Vote." *TIME*, May 8, 2016. http://fortune.com/2016/05/08/uber-lyft-leaving-austin/.

Dua, Tanya. "Brands Are Counseling the Young and the Traumatized through Their #Quarterlifecrisis." *Digiday*, June 14, 2016. http://digiday.com/brands/brands-counseling-millennials-quarterlife-crises/.

Dua, Tanya. "Kik Me Some Lipstick: Sephora Bets on Messaging Apps for E-Commerce." *DigiDay*, March 31, 2016. http://digiday.com/brands/see-kik-sephora-bets-messaging-apps-e-commerce/.

Dykstra, Josh Allan. "Why Millennials Don't Want to Buy Stuff." *Fast Company*, July 13, 2012. www.fastcompany.com/1842581/why-millennials-dont-want-buy-stuff.

Eventbrite. "Millennials: Fueling the Experience Economy." November 20, 2016. http://eventbrite-s3.s3.amazonaws.com/marketing/Millennials_Research/Gen_PR_Final.pdf.

EY. *Competition, Coexistence or Symbiosis? The DNA of C-Suite Sales and Marketing Leaders the CMO Perspective*. London: EY, 2014.

Fast Company. "Most Innovative Companies." November 20, 2016. www.fastcompany.com/most-innovative-companies.

Fast Company. "Netflix." November 20, 2016. www.fastcompany.com/company/netflix.

Fitzpatrick, Alex. "Airline: 70,000 Passengers Missed Flights Due to Security Lines." *Time*, May 26, 2016. http://time.com/4349766/airline-70000-passengers-missed-flights-due-to-security-lines/.

Fred, Lambert. "Tesla v8.0 Software Update Is Being Pushed Right Now, All the Details and Full Release Notes." *Electrek*, September 22, 2016. https://electrek.co/2016/09/22/tesla-v8-0-software-update-is-being-pushed-right-now-all-the-details-and-full-release-notes/.

Frumkin, Tamar. "5 Ways Millennials Are Re-Defining the Customer Experience." *Sales Force*, April 9, 2015. www.salesforce.com/blog/2015/04/5-ways-millennials-re-defining-customer-experience-gp.html.

Fry, Richard. "For First Time in Modern Era, Living with Parents Edges out Other Living Arrangements for 18- to 34-Year-Olds." *Pew Research Center*, May 24, 2016. www.pewsocialtrends.org/2016/05/24/for-first-time-in-modern-era-living-with-parents-edges-out-other-living-arrangements-for-18-to-34-year-olds/.

Gallup. "Employee Engagement in U.S. Stagnant in 2015." January 13, 2016. www.gallup.com/poll/188144/employee-engagement-stagnant-2015.aspx.

Generational Research Foundation. "Generation X." November 21, 2016. www.generationalresearchfoundation.com/generation-x.

Genesys. "The Value of Experience: How the C-Suite Values Customer Experience in the Digital Age Global & North America Executive Summary." November 19, 2016. www.genesys.com/about/resources/the-value-of-experience-how-the-c-suite-values-customer-experience-in-the-digital-age-na.

Goodman, John A. *Customer Experience 3*. 1st ed. New York: AMACOM, 2014.

Griffith, Erin. "Brands Are Using Social Media More Than Ever, and Users Are Ignoring Them More Than Ever." *Fortune*, August 25, 2016. http://fortune.com/2015/08/25/social-media-brands-ignore/.

Griffith, Erin. "Content, Commerce, and Cooking: How Food52 Is Making Small Community into a Big Business." *Fortune*, August 7, 2014. http://fortune.com/2014/08/07/content-commerce-cooking-food52/.

Groden, Claire. "Here's How Many Americans Sleep with Their Smartphones." *Fortune*, June 29, 2015. http://fortune.com/2015/06/29/sleep-banks-smartphones/.

Haddon, Heather, "Attention Shoppers: Yoga in Aisle 3," *Wall Street Journal*, June 13, 2016. https://www.wsj.com/articles/attention-shoppers-yoga-in-aisle-3-1465860325.

Hagberg, Eva. "Rooms with a View." *Metropolis*, December 2013. www.metropolismag.com/December-2013/Rooms-with-a-View/index.php?cparticle=3&siarticle=2#artanc.

Hamari, Juho, Mimmi Sjöklint, and Antti Ukkonen. "The Sharing Economy: Why People Participate in Collaborative Consumption." *Journal of the Association for Information Science and Technology* 67, no. 9 (2015): 2047–2059. doi:10.1002/asi.23552.

Handleman, Ben. "Class Action Lawsuit: Wisconsin Uber Drivers Sue Uber." *FOX 6 Now*, June 24, 2016. http://fox6now.com/2016/06/24/class-action-lawsuit-wisconsin-uber-drivers-sue-uber.

The Happiness Project. "Podcast 64: Go Slow to Go Fast; What Do You Lie about; and a New Segment—the 'Happiness Hack'." Last modified May 11, 2016. http://gretchenrubin.com/happiness_project/2016/05/podcast-64/.

Hosain, Syed Zaeem. "Reality Check: 50B IoT Devices Connected by 2020: Beyond the Hype and into Reality." *RSR Wireless News*, June 28, 2016. www.rcrwireless.com/20160628/opinion/reality-check-50b-iot-devices-connected-2020-beyond-hype-reality-tag10.

Housel, Morgan. "The 20 Smartest Things Jeff Bezos Has Ever Said." *The Motley Fool*, September 9, 2013. www.fool.com/investing/general/2013/09/09/the-25-smartest-things-jeff-bezos-has-ever-said.aspx.

Howe, Neil. "Why Millennials Are Texting More and Talking Less." *Forbes*, July 15, 2015. www.forbes.com/sites/neilhowe/2015/07/15/why-millennials-are-texting-more-and-talking-less/#4cc637965576.

Hyman, Julie. "Women Make up 85% of All Consumer Purchases." *Bloomberg*, July 22, 2016. www.bloomberg.com/news/videos/b/9e28517f-8de1–4e59-bcda-ce536aa50bd6.

IBM. "How IBM Watson Inspired Alex Da Kid's New Song 'Not Easy'." *Business Insider*, October 25, 2016. www.businessinsider.com/sc/ibm-watson-helps-create-alex-da-kid-song-2016–10.

Iudica, David. (Senior Director Strategic Insights & Research, Yahoo), in discussion with the author.

Jacobson, Roni. "How Snapchat's Sponsored Lenses Became a Money-Printing Machine." *Back Channel*, October 21, 2016. https://backchannel.com/how-snapchats-sponsored-lenses-became-a-money-printing-machine-a1e45b0a82b#.mij9j4zcv.

Khan, Humayun. "Why Run a Pop-Up?" *Shopify*, November 21, 2016. www.shopify.com/guides/ultimate-guide-to-pop-up-shops/why-run-a-pop-up.

Kleinschmit, Matt. "Generation Z Characteristics: 5 Infographics on the Gen Z Lifestyle." *Vision Critical Communications*, December 4, 2015. www.visioncritical.com/generation-z-infographics.

LaCapria, Kim. "Zulily Rejects Winter Coat Return, Suggests Donating It to the Needy." *Urban Legends Reference Pages*, January 13, 2016. www.snopes.com/2016/01/13/zulily-rejects-winter-coat/#.

Laghaei, Jamshid, Ardeshir Faghri, and Mingxin Li. "Impacts of Home Shopping on Vehicle Operations and Greenhouse Gas Emissions: Multi-Year Regional Study." *International Journal of Sustainable Development & World Ecology* 23, no. 5 (2015): 381–391. doi:10.1080/13504509.2015.1124471.

Langley, Monica. "Salesforce's Marc Benioff Has Kicked off New Era of Corporate Social Activism." *The Wall Street Journal*, May 2, 2016. www.wsj.com/articles/salesforces-marc-benioff-has-kicked-off-new-era-of-corporate-social-activism-1462201172.

Lashinsky, Adam. "Amazon's Jeff Bezos: The Ultimate Disrupter." *Fortune*, November 16, 2012. http://fortune.com/2012/11/16/amazons-jeff-bezos-the-ultimate-disrupter/.

Lavoie, Andre. "4 Reasons You Need to Embrace Transparency in the Workplace." *Entrepreneur*, April 28, 2015. www.entrepreneur.com/article/245461.

Lazovick, Meg. "Wake Me Up: What Time Do Americans Start Their Day?" *Edison Research*, March 26, 2015. www.edisonresearch.com/wake-me-up-series-2/.

Leggett, Kate. "Forrester's Top Trends for Customer Service in 2015." *Forrester*, December 17, 2014. http://blogs.forrester.com/kate_leggett/14–12–17-forresters_top_trends_for_customer_service_in_2015.

Lenhart, Amanda. "Cell Phone Ownership." *Pew Research Center*, March 19, 2012. www.pewinternet.org/2012/03/19/cell-phone-ownership/.

Lewis, Julia. "How to Deliver Exceptional Service to Four Generations of Customers." *Provide Support*, April 16, 2015. www.providesupport.com/blog/four-generations-of-customers.

Lovinus, Adam. "B2B E-Commerce: Shop with a Phone, Buy with a Desktop?" *Newegg Business*, July 16, 2015. https://blog.neweggbusiness.com/trends/b2b-e-commerce-shop-with-a-phone-buy-with-a-desktop/.

Ma, Michelle. "Grocery Delivery Service Is Greener Than Driving to the Store." *University of Washington Today*, April 29, 2013. www.washington.edu/news/2013/04/29/grocery-delivery-service-is-greener-than-driving-to-the-store/.

Mac, Ryan. "Stitch Fix: The $250 Million Startup Playing Fashionista Moneyball." *Forbes*, June 1, 2016. www.forbes.com/sites/ryanmac/2016/06/01/fashionista-moneyball-stitch-fix-katrina-lake/#549c2a662e2e.

McCaskill, Andrew. "Consumer-Goods' Brands That Demonstrate Commitment to Sustainability Outperform Those That Don't." *Nielsen.Com*, October 12, 2015. www.nielsen.com/us/en/press-room/2015/consumer-goods-brands-that-demonstrate-commitment-to-sustainability-outperform.html.

McDonald, Kelly. *Crafting the Customer Experience for People Not Like You: How to Delight and Engage the Customers Your Competitors Don't Understand*. Hoboken, NJ: Wiley & Sons, 2013.

Maney, Kevin. "Why Milennials Still Move to Cites." *Newsweek*, March 30, 2015. www.newsweek.com/2015/04/10/why-cities-hold-more-pull-millennials-cloud-317735.html.

Mann, Annamarie and Jim Harter. "The Worldwide Employee Engagement Crisis." *Gallup Business Journal*, January 7, 2016. www.gallup.com/businessjournal/188033/worldwide-employee-engagement-crisis.aspx.

Martin, Roger. "The Age of Customer Capitalism." *Harvard Business Review*, January–February 2010 Issue. https://hbr.org/2010/01/the-age-of-customer-capitalism.

Marvin, Ginny. "Salesforce Gets into Internet of Things Market with IoT Cloud." *Marketing Land*, September 15, 2015. http://marketingland.com/salesforce-gets-into-internet-of-things-market-with-iot-cloud-142684.

Meeker, Mary. "Internet Trends 2016." *KPCB*, June 1, 2016. www.kpcb.com/blog/2016-internet-trends-report.

Meola, Andrew. "Long Wait Times on the Phone with Customer Service May Be a Thing of the Past." *Business Insider*, July 1, 2016. www.businessinsider.com/long-wait-times-on-the-phone-with-customer-service-may-be-a-thing-of-the-past-2016-7.

Minutemen. "Increasing Churn Rate in the S&P 500: What's the Lifespan of Your Stock?" *Seeking Alpha*, November 6, 2014. http://seekingalpha.com/article/2651195-increasing-churn-rate-in-the-s-and-p-500-whats-the-lifespan-of-your-stock.

Morgan, Blake. *A Practitioner's View: 20 Top Brands Address Their Challenges with the Customer Experience Vendor Landscape.* Oakland: Self published, 2016.

Morgan, Jacob. "Why the Future of Our Organizations Depends on Having More Women in Management." *Forbes*, February 18, 2015. www.forbes.com/sites/jacobmorgan/2015/02/18/why-the-future-of-our-organizations-depends-on-having-more-women-in-management/#1502abe266a8.

Meyer, Christopher and Schwager, Andre, "Understanding Customer Experience," *Harvard Business Review*, February 2007. https://hbr.org/2007/02/understanding-customer-experience.

O'Connor, Clare. "Nasty Gal's Sophia Amoruso Hits Richest Self-Made Women List with $280 Million Fortune." *Forbes*, June 1, 2016. www.forbes.com/sites/clareoconnor/2016/06/01/nasty-gal-sophia-amoruso-richest-women-net-worth/#65290a9044e1.

O'Connor, Kevin. "Personas: The Foundation of a Great User Experience." *UX Magazine*, March 25, 2011. https://uxmag.com/articles/personas-the-foundation-of-a-great-user-experience.

Paquette, Aaron. "Ad Blocking and Teen Engagement: Here's What Marketers Need to Know." *MediaPost Communications*, October 8, 2015. www.mediapost.com/publications/article/260049/ad-blocking-and-teen-engagement-heres-what-marke.html.

Paul, Jasmine. "Marketing to Millennials? Meh. The Future Is Gen Z." *Mad Fish Digital*, July 20, 2016. www.madfishdigital.com/blog/genz-marketing-millennials/.

Peart, Nick. "2014: The Year of Omnichannel Customer Service." *ZenDesk*, November 25, 2013. www.zendesk.com/blog/omnichannel-2014.

The Pew Charitable Trusts. *Economic Mobility: Is the American Dream Alive and Well?* 1st ed. Philadelphia: The Pew Charitable Trusts, 2007.

Price, Shayla. "Why Customer-Focused Content Should Be a Priority." *Marketing Media Insider*, February 15, 2016. https://marketinginsidergroup.com/content-marketing/customer-focused-content-priority/.

Pride, Ray. "Work Out as Little as You Want: Netflix, Ron Howard and White-Water Kayaking." *MSN Blogs*, December 18, 2006. http://moviecitynews.com/2006/12/work-out-as-little-as-you-want-netflix-ron-howard-and-white-water-kayaking/.

Reason, Ben, Lovlie, Lavrans, and Flu Brand, Melvin, *Service Design for Business: A Practical Guide to Optimizing Experience.*

Rein, Lisa. "Veteran Preference in Federal Hiring: The 'Third Rail of Civil Service Reform' Expert Says." *The Washington Post*, June 27, 2016. www.washingtonpost.

com/news/powerpost/wp/2016/06/27/veteran-preference-in-federal-hiring-the-third-rail-of-civil-service-reform-expert-says.

Richtel, Matt. "E-Commerce: Convenience Built on a Mountain of Cardboard." *The New York Times Company*, February 16, 2016. www.nytimes.com/2016/02/16/science/recycling-cardboard-online-shopping-environment.html.

Rosoff, Matt. "More Than Half of Americans Will Do 'Most' of Their Holiday Shopping at Amazon." *Business Insider*, December 17, 2015. www.businessinsider.com/amazon-dominates-holiday-shopping-2015–12?utm_source=feedly&utm_medium=webfeeds.

Rossman, John. *The Amazon Way: 14 Leadership Principles behind the World's Most Disruptive Company*. CreateSpace Independent Publishing Platform, 2014.

Seemiller, Corey and Meghan Grace. *Generation Z Goes to College*. 1st ed. San Francisco: Jossey-Bass, 2016.

Shahrokhi, Bijan. "Here's How Facebook Messenger Will Change Banking." *Venture Beat*, June 5, 2016. http://venturebeat.com/2016/06/05/say-hello-to-messenger-banking/.

Shaul, Brandy. "Flurry: Time Spent on Phablets Increased 334% in 2015." *Social Times*, January 5, 2016. www.adweek.com/socialtimes/flurry-time-spent-on-phablets-increased-334-in-2015/632374.

Shen, Lucinda. "Amazon's Stock Just Hit a Major Milestone." *Fortune*, September 22, 2016. http://fortune.com/2016/09/22/amazon-stock-history/.

Shi, Audrey. "Amazon Prime Members Now Outnumber Non-Prime Customers." *Fortune*, July 11, 2016. http://fortune.com/2016/07/11/amazon-prime-customers/.

Shontell, Alyson. "If You Think It's Crazy That Snapchat Might Go Public at a $40 Billion Valuation, Here's Something to Consider." *Business Insider*, November 1, 2016. www.businessinsider.com/is-snapchat-ipo-worth-investing-in-2016–10.

Sims, David. "Silicon Valley's Sad Ballad of Start-Up Success." *The Atlantic Monthly Group*, May 2, 2016. www.theatlantic.com/entertainment/archive/2016/05/silicon-valleys-sad-ballad-of-tech-success/480849/.

Slodysko, Brian. "Survey: Religious Objections Law Cost Indiana as Much as $60 Million." *The Chicago Tribune*, January 26, 2016. www.chicagotribune.com/news/local/breaking/ct-survey-religious-objections-law-cost-indiana-as-much-as-60-million-20160126-story.html.

Smith, Craig. "By the Numbers: 20 Important Kik Messenger Stats." *DMR*, August 25, 2016. http://expandedramblings.com/index.php/kik-messenger-stats/.

Solis, Brian, *X: The Experience When Business Meets Design*. Hoboken, New Jersey, John Wiley & Sons, 2015.

Son, Hugh and Claire Boston. "Dimon Says CEOs Should Focus More on Long Term, Not Analysts." *Bloomberg*, October 19, 2015. www.bloomberg.com/news/articles/2015–10–19/dimon-says-ceos-should-abstain-from-giving-guidance-on-earnings.

Sozzi, Brian. "20 Reasons Why Sears Is the Worst Stock in the World." *The Street*, February 2, 2016. www.thestreet.com/story/13444692/1/20-reasons-why-sears-is-the-worst-stock-in-the-world.html.

Syrett, Alison, Fashionista.com, "How Millennial Labels Are Bringing Brand Loyalty Back," June 14, 2016. http://fashionista.com/2016/06/brand-loyalty-millennials.

Taft, Darryl. "IBM's Rometty Takes Watson to CES." *Declara*, January 6, 2016. https://declara.com/content/A5YOqw21.

Topolsky, Joshua. "The End of Twitter." *New Yorker*, January 29, 2016. www.newyorker.com/tech/elements/the-end-of-twitter.

Trust, Gary. "Alex Da Kid Hits Rock Charts with Watson BEAT Collab 'Not Easy'." *Billboard*, March 11, 2016. www.billboard.com/articles/columns/chart-beat/7565454/alex-da-kid-rock-charts-watson-beat-not-easy.

Tynan, Dan. "Sephora, Neiman Marcus Turn to In-Store Technology to Enhance the Retail Experience." *Biz Tech*, June 2, 2016. www.biztechmagazine.com/article/2016/06/sephora-neiman-marcus-turn-store-technology-enhance-retail-experience.

Tyson, Matthew. "Millennials Want Brands to Be More Authentic: Here's Why That Matters." *The Huffington Post*, January 21, 2016. www.huffingtonpost.com/matthew-tyson/millennials-want-brands-t_b_9032718.html.

Visser, Susan. "5 Disruptive Technologies That Are Challenging the Traditional Banking Model." *IBM Big Data and Analytics Hub*, May 16, 2016. www.ibmbigdatahub.com/blog/5-disruptive-technologies-are-challenging-traditional-banking-model.

Waggoner, John. "Do Happy Workers Mean Higher Company Profits?" *USA Today*, February 20, 2013. www.usatoday.com/story/money/personal-finance/2013/02/19/treating-employees-well-stock-price/1839887/.

Weinstein, Mark. (SVP and Global Head of Customer Engagement, Loyalty and Partnerships for Hilton Worldwide), in discussion with the author.

Wilson, Craig, *The Compass and the Nail: How the Patagonia Model of Loyalty Can Save Your Business, and Might Just Save the Planet*, Los Angeles, Vireo/Rare Bird, 2015.

Wong, Curtis M. "Indiana's Memories Pizza Reportedly Becomes First Business to Reject Catering Gay Weddings." *Huffington Post*, April 1, 2015. www.huffingtonpost.com/2015/04/01/indiana-pizza-gay-couples_n_6985208.html.

Zonkel, Phillip. "AIDS Crisis Loomed over Generation X." *Long Beac1h Press Telegram*, February 1, 2016. www.presstelegram.com/health/20160102/aids-crisis-loomed-over-generation-x.

Index

1-800-Flowers 22

Absolut 33
access vs. ownership 12, 148–52
adventure seeking 107–8
Airbnb 36–8, 73–5
air travel 173–4
Alex Da Kid 31
Altiux 34
Amazon: business transformation process 130; digital experience of 57; earnings 17; innovations of 63–4; invent and simplify leadership principle 63–4; long-term gains focus 172; performance gap 164–5; virtual assistant 164
Amazon Echo 164
Amazon Fresh 129
Amazon Go 46
Amazon Prime 108, 163
Amazon returns 163
Amazon Web Services (AWS) 64
American Airlines 58
American Psychological Association 136

Amoruso, Sophia 111
Annual Chief Customer Office Study 8
anti-consumerist philosophy 12
Apple 43, 94, 130
artificial intelligence 30–1
Ashley Madison 42
Atkinson, Graham 8–9
Avon 125

baby boomers 143, 154–5
bad profits 172–3
Baer, Jay 16
banking 22–3
banner blindness 51
Basulto, David 18
Benioff, Marc 97, 98
Bezos, Jeff 57, 93, 101–2, 163, 164, 172
binge watching 66
blended teams 80–1, 91
Bliss, Jeanne 8–9
Blockbuster 64–6
Bodine, Kerry 95
Box 78
brands: accountable for customer experience 74; buyers interacting with

15–16; controlling approach to social media 24, 89; illusory superiority of 11–13; mass advertising of 50; mobile experience 17

Branson, Richard 60

Burke, Robert 146

businesses: bad profits 172–3; business transformation process 130–1; creating customer experience standards 95–6; culture and engagement as top challenge 71; customer effort framework 131–3; desktop experience vs. mobile experiences of 17; diversity on board of 100; earnings focus of 171; embracing disruption 111–14; environmental footprint 101–2; flexible work arrangements 62–3; governance within 95–6; human duct tape of 8–9; innovative 110; investing in workplace 71–3; long-term performance 171; preserving environment 96–7; social activism of 97–9; social responsibility 100; stakeholder accountability 95; structure 10–11; sustainable practices of 102–4; three-horizon framework 109–12

business transformation process 130–1

Canada Post 96

CEOs (chief executive officers): activist role of 97–9; employee satisfaction and 72–3; engaging with employees 9–10; leading by example 9; owning customer experience 7; short-term profits focus of 171

channels, communication: for customer service 87–9; personalization in 127; proper support for 165–6; serving customers in preferred 23–4; see also social media

chatbots 17, 21–2

Chesky, Brian 37, 74, 141

chief customer officer 8–9

Chief Customer Officer (Bliss) 8–9

Chief Customer Officer Council 8–9

chief executive officers see CEOs (chief executive officers)

Cisco 31–2

Clarabridge 138

collaboration tool 127

Collective Disruption: How Corporations & Startups Can Co-Create Transformative New Businesses (Docherty) 108–9

commoditization 5

communication: among millennials 90; change management and 135; changing modes of 7; customer's use of technology 23; disruption in 115; e-mail 87–8; Facebook Messenger for 20–1; one-way 174; text messaging as dominant form of 90; see also channels, communication

companies see businesses

Compass and the Nail, The: How the Patagonia Model of Loyalty Can Save Your Business, and Might Just Save the Planet (Wilson) 102, 151

complacency 12, 64–6

consumer choice 102

contact centers: employee dissatisfaction and 72; as relationship-building tool 25; service recovery in 70; staffing 103; streamlining 91

Cook, Tim 97

core business transformation 130

corporations *see* businesses

Craft, The (blog) 117–18

CRM (customer relationship management) technology 78–80, 166–8

C-suite perspective on listening 3–4

curiosity 138–9

customer acquisition 125

customer-centricity 10, 94

customer delight: impacting company's internal culture 159; saving time 162–3; service recovery programs and 160–1

customer effort 131–3

customer engagement: Avon and 125; on Facebook 20–1; Kik Interactive 17–18; Sephora 17–18; on Snapchat 18–19

customer experience: brands not in control of 5–6; crisis in 5; critical to brand building 72–3; defined 84–5, 123–7; happiness levels affecting 69–70; influenced by companies 124; operational view of 125–6; partial ownership of 7–8; performance gap in 163–6; as reflection of employee experience 72–3; responsibility for 6–8; social responsibility and 100; technology to enhance 28; user experience vs.

84–5; with wearable technology 28–30

Customer Experience 3.0 (Goodman) 4

customer-facing staff 70

customer-focused teams, hiring practices for 137–41

customer loyalty 93–4

customer perception 124

customer relationship management (CRM) technology 78–80

customers: achieving their goals 125–8; comparing company experiences 16; expectations of 15; finding content 90–1; interacting with brands 15–16; internal departments collaborating around 126; who don't complain 94

customer service: channels 87–9; evolution of 85–6; new names for 92; operational hours 87; technology making experience worse 86–7; *see also* customer experience

Da Kid, Alex 31

data-cleansing process 45

data management 45

data privacy 43–4

data security 42–3

Delight Center 61–2

delight programs 160

Dell, Michael 138

Denning, Steve 172–3

design thinking 73–4

digital start-ups 114

Dimon, Jamie 171

Dirty Jobs (TV show) 139

Discovery Channel 139
Disney MagicBand 28–9
disruption: based on communication
   115–17; companies embracing
   111–14
Dixon, Matthew 159
Docherty, Michael 108–9
drones 101–2
Dykstra, Josh 151

eBay 63–4
e-commerce platform 23, 64
Edelman, David 125–7
*Effortless Experience, The: Conquering
   the New Battleground for Customer
   Loyalty* (Dixon) 5
employee-focused cultures 137
employees: can-do attitude 139;
   dissatisfaction of 72; down-to-earth
   attitude 140–1; empowering 70;
   engagement of 69, 71, 137; innate
   curiosity 138–9; as intrapreneurs
   138–9; promotional opportunities
   136; stress 135; team-oriented
   attitude 140; technology-savvy
   139–40; trust in their employer 136
energy management 34–5
environment: carbon footprint
   101–2; hiring practices and 103–5;
   millennials and 151–2; packaging
   waste 102
Ernst & Young survey 3
experience architecture 28–9
experience-driven industries 107
Experience Economy, The (Gilmore) 107
Experience Economy, The (Pine)
   128–30

Facebook 19–20, 110, 116
Facebook Messenger 20–3
Faghri, Ardeshi 101
fashion start-ups 149–50
FBI (Federal Bureau of Investigation)
   43
feedback 4
Feller, Frerk-Malte 21
female consumers 100
first-call resolution 161
Fitbit 29, 31, 32
Food52 115–17
Fortune magazine 115
Fox, Jodie 60
friction, between customers and
   business 55–6
Fulfillment by Amazon (FBA) services
   64, 110

Gaikwad, Siddharth 47–8
Gallup 69, 71, 90
Ganeshan, Susan 138
Gebauer, Julie 71
Gebbia, Joe 74
GE Capital 172
generational studies 143
Generation X 152–4
*Generation X Goes Global: Mapping a
   Youth Culture in Motion* (Henseler)
   153
Generation Z: access vs. ownership
   12; company's social activism and
   99; comparison shopping of 16–17;
   customer experiences for 144–6;
   defined 144; marketing to 145; text
   messaging of 90
Genesys 7

Gilmore, James 107, 128–30
#*Girlboss* (Amoruso) 111
global environmental issues 151–2
GoDaddy 80
Goodman, John 4, 123–4
Google 71, 130
GPS apps 49
Griffith, Erin 51
grocery chains 128–9
growth horizons 109–12

hackers 42–3
Hansen, Marka 150
Harris Interactive 146–7
Hastings, Reed 65
Hello Barbie 33–4
Henseler, Christine 153
Herrin, Jessica 61, 125, 141
Hilton Worldwide 124, 160
hiring practices 103–5, 137–41
Hoback, Cullen 44
Hyatt 79

IBM 30
Illiason, Robert 27
illusory superiority 11–13
innovative companies 110
Innovator's DNA, The (Christensen)
    138
insertion strategy 50–2
Instagram 51
instant gratification 147, 154
instant messaging 87
interactive voice response (IVR)
    technology 86–7
Internet of Things (IoT): content
    finding customers through 90–1;
defined 31–2; device 29; embedded
    80; IoT Cloud 32; products 33–4;
    solving performance gap 168
intrapreneurs 138–9
iOgrapher 18
IoT Cloud 32
iPhone 43

JackThreads 20–1
just-in-time messaging 4–5, 35

Kik Interactive 17–18
Kinkel, Kelly Blue 161–2
Kurzweil, Ray 143

Le Tote 149
Levchin, Max 97
Levie, Aaron 78
listening 3
Louis CK 41
Luddites 140
Lululemon 114
Luxe Valet 141
Lyft 74–5

McCann, Chris 22
McDonald, Kelly 155
machine learning 46–7; *see also*
    artificial intelligence
Manning, Harley 95
marketers/marketing: collaborating
    with internal departments 126–7;
    ill-timed 49–50; "insertion"
    approach 50–2; personalization in
    51–2; short-form visual 145
Martin, Roger 172
mass messaging 49–50

Mattel 33–4
meal delivery services 129
mediocrity 5
Meeker, Mary 35, 43
messaging: instant 87; mass 49–50;
    one-size-fits-all 4–5; tailored 4–5;
    text 90; *see also* communication
messaging apps 90
Meyer, Christopher 127
Michaels 114
Microsoft Bot Framework 23
Microsoft Cloud 113–14
millennials: access vs. ownership 147,
    148–52; company's social activism
    and 99; defined 146; engagement
    of 152; experiences vs. ownership
    146–7; following *The Craft* 117–18;
    on global environmental issues
    151–2; instant gratification and 147;
    quarter-life crisis theme 150; text
    messaging of 90; trusted circles 150
Moriarty, Dan 79

Näraffär 27
Nasty Gal 111
NCAA (National Collegiate Athletic
    Association) 97–8
Nest Learning Thermostat 34–5
Netflix 50, 65–6
"next best action" 48–9; *see also*
    personas
Nielsen 151
Nordstrom 83–4
Notaro, Tig 41

omnichannel approach 89, 178
on-demand economy 25, 35–6,
    59–60, 75, 117–18

on-demand workers 103–4
one-size-fits-all messaging 4–5
one-way communication 174
online fashion start-ups 149–50
operational business transformation 130
organizations; *see* businesses
*Outside In: The Power of Putting
    Customers at the Center of Your
    Business* (Bodine) 95–6

packaging waste 102
Pegasystems 77
Pepper 30
performance gap in customer
    experience 163–6
personalization 51–2, 127
personas 47–9
phablet 24
Pine, Joseph 107, 128–30
Pinterest 51
Pizza Hut 30
pop-up shops 114
Potter, Jeff 57–9
predictive model 48–9
product recall 32
products, self-diagnosing software
    32–3
"propensity to buy or use" 48–9;
    see also personas
Pure Software 65

Real Madrid 46–7
Rechterman, Barb 80
Reichheld, Fred 172–3
Religious Freedom Restoration Act
    (Indiana) 97–8
retail store: changing role of 112–14;
    pop-up shops 114

return policies 83–4
Rhodin, Mike 31
robots 30–1, 46
Rosser, Jason 20–1
Rossman, John 63
Rover app 35
Rowe, Mike 139

Salesforce 32, 97
Schultz, Howard 99
Schwager, Andre 127
seamless experience 127
Sears Holdings 112
security breaches 42–3
self-service technologies 27–8
Sephora 17–18, 113
Service Design for Business: A Practical Guide to Optimizing the Customer Experience (Reason) 55–6, 70
service recovery 70, 93–4, 160–1
sharing economy 25, 35; *see also* on-demand economy
Shoes of Prey 59–61
Silicon Valley (television series) 171
Simple Storage Service 64
Sinek, Simon 126
single market messaging 4–5
"Six Rings of the Modern Customer Experience, The" 127–8
smart bottle technology 33
smart cities 34
Snapchat 18–19
social activism 97–9
social customer service 166–7
social media: baby boomers and 154; customer engagement on 18–21; customer service operational hours and 87; Facebook 19–21, 110, 116; Snapchat 18–19; Twitter 48
social responsibility 100
software-defined society 43–5
Solis, Brian 28–9
Sony Pictures Entertainment 42–3
Southworth, Devaraj 118
Sports Authority 112
stakeholders 127
Stalk, George 162–3
start-ups: digital 114; online fashion 149–50
Start with Why (Sinek) 126
Staten, James 113–14
Stella & Dot family of brands 61–4, 125
Stitch Fix 114, 149–50
Stoppelman, Jeremy 97
"Stop Trying to Delight Your Customers" (Dixon) 159
storytelling 146
strategic business transformation 130
Stubbs, Merrill 116–17
Surf Air 57–9
sustainable practices 102–4

tailored content 18
Target 64
team-oriented attitude 140
technology: architecture from business perspective 77; baby boomers and 154; blended teams and 80–1; curse of old 78–9; effect on employee experience 78; interactive voice response 86–7; limits on seamless operations 78–9; machine learning 46–7; making experience worse 86–7; personalized telephone support 80; security breaches 42–3;

self-diagnosing software 33; self-service 27–8; terms and conditions 44–5; turnkey 79; wearable 28–30
TechTarget 32
Tercek, Robert 43, 44
terms and conditions 44–5
Terms and Conditions May Apply (documentary) 44
Tesla Motors 33
text messaging 90
theSkimm (newsletter) 150
Thirstie 117–18
Toman, Nick 159
Tondon, Rakesh 149
Topolsky, Joshua 19–20
Towers Watson 71
Toys "R" Us 64
transformative innovation 110
transparency in the workplace 45, 137
Trefler, Alan 77
turnkey technology 79
Twitter 48

Uber 74–5
Ultimate Question, The (Reichheld) 172–3
Undercover Boss (TV show) 9–10, 61–2, 141
USA Today (newspaper) 71
user experience vs. customer experience 84–5
UX Magazine 47

value creation 128
venture-backed companies 149–50
Venture Beat 22–3
Veterans 103
visual marketing 145

Wall Street Journal 116
Warby Parker 102–3
Waterson, Sheree 111
Watson 30
Waze 49–50
wearable technology 28–30, 31
WeddingChannel.com 125
Weinstein, Mark 124, 160
Welch, Jack 172
"What Is Customer Experience?" (article) 127
"Why Millennials Don't Buy Stuff" (Dykstra) 151
Wilson, Craig 102, 151
WordPress 48
WorkFlex solutions 104

X: The Experience When Business Meets Design (Solis) 28–9

YouTube stars 145

Zappos 84
Zuckerberg, Mark 21–2
Zulily 161–2

About the Author

Blake Morgan is an author, speaker, and globally recognized thought leader on customer experience. She's worked with brands such as Intel, Verizon, Newmark Knight Frank Retail, the largest Chinese sharing economy company, and many vendors in the customer experience space. She has a regular column on *Forbes*, a popular podcast called *The Modern Customer* and a weekly YouTube series where she looks at the future of customer experience. She's a highly sought-after speaker and workshop leader, and frequently works with customer experience vendors on thought leadership programs. She lives in *Alameda*, California, with her husband, daughter, and two dogs.

Visit Blake at www.blakemichellemorgan.com.